Ceremonies of Innocence:

Essays from the Indian Wars

STEVE RUSSELL

Published by

Dog Iron Press

127 Blazing Star Drive

Georgetown, TX 78633

ISBN: 1481125745
ISBN-13: 9781481125741

TO THE EDITORIAL STAFF OF *INDIAN COUNTRY TODAY*,

where much of this material first appeared,

who put up with my quirks for years:

Randi Rourke-Barreiro

Ray Cook

Chris Napolitano

Matt DeMazza

Bob Roe

and all the Indian intellectuals

who dare not speak the name

intellectual

but make me appear smarter than I am

because of the distance I can describe

from standing on their shoulders.

And to my wife Tracy

who put up with even more quirks

for even more years

and makes me appear more organized than I am.

The blood-dimmed tide is loosed, and everywhere

The ceremony of innocence is drowned;

The best lack all conviction, while the worst

Are full of passionate intensity.

---William Butler Yeats

CONTENTS

1 SOVEREIGNTY AND ELECTIONS

Sovereignty is not what it used to be, and I am not speaking of Indian sovereignty in particular. Sometimes I think about the rise of the nation-state with bemusement at the customs of historians. That rise is marked from the Treaty of Westphalia in 1648, but the feudal subjects who were the vast majority of humanity could certainly see no difference at the time.

It was the rulers who had their actions constrained, much like the Magna Carta constrained the English king in a manner that made a world of difference in theory but not a hill of beans to the average Englishwoman.

Westphalia allegedly defined sovereignty of states and recognized the political equality of all states, as well as a concomitant duty of each state not to interfere in the internal affairs of another. These constraints were and are violated on many pretexts, but they represent a baseline expectation that creates political leverage against violators.

In virtually all nation-states of the time, "sovereignty" resided in the person of the sovereign, the monarch, who ruled either by inheritance or by force of arms. All decisions of government were personal decisions of one individual, with all the human variation that implies.

Criminal law arose to punish a violation of "the King's peace," and what disturbed the King's peace was whatever the King decided from time to time. El Camino Real, "the King's Highway," was an established trade route where any robbers were on advance notice that robbery would disturb the King's peace, and by robbing in that place they made themselves outlaw—their property and their lives forfeited.

Westphalian sovereignty did not address methods of government, and a common pretext for intervention in the internal affairs of other nations came with the often-bloody decline of monarchies. The royal families of Europe were intermarried to a degree that concentrated their political interests along with their recessive genetic traits.

Those royals who survive today are heads of state, not heads of government, and there is a rough division between nations of democratic form and nations of authoritarian form. Most nations have aspects of both, just as virtually all modern economies blend capitalism with socialism.

American Indians need to note that date historians pick for the rise of the modern nation-state, 1648. The idea that all European governments were more advanced than all governments indigenous to the Americas at the time Columbus got lost is fairly preposterous.

We had monarchies just like Europe's, but also pure democracies, various kinds of confederations, and theocracies. The Six Nations had famously solved the riddle of representation by geographical area and by population, whether or not Ben Franklin brought that into the writing of the US Constitution. There is plenty of physical evidence that pre-Columbian trade routes spanned the entire continent. Trade on that scale does not take place without political organization sufficient to guarantee the peace.

To say that European diseases decimated Indian nations would be absurd understatement, since to "decimate" is literally to kill one in ten. There is no hard count of the Indian nations lost to history. The US colonial government currently recognizes between five and six hundred remaining, but many of those are fragments of peoples who used to be one. My own nation is divided into three pieces by various accidents of colonial history.

My people progressed from theocracy to monarchy to confederated towns. We became a constitutional republic in 1827, making our republic older than many of those recognized by the United Nations. The most common form of tribal government in the US is by a "constitution" pulled off the shelf at the Bureau of Indian Affairs. Chiefs are weak, tribal councils are elected boards of directors, and tribal courts are tacked on afterthoughts.

Indian government forms are not sitting still, but neither is the context in which they function. Nation-states are bleeding authority in both directions. From below, there are regional demands for self-government and delegations of authority to state, county, and municipal governments as well as special purpose units with varying degrees of autonomy.

From above, there are webs of multi-lateral treaties that have attached to the skeleton that was customary international law. There are the institutions growing from that body, such as the Permanent International Court of Justice and the numerous special purpose courts that have managed to put former heads of government in the dock for crimes against humanity. There is the UN Security Council, which is authorized to use military force against outlaw nations.

The nation-state is in the process of being supplanted by the transnational corporation as the dominant form of human political organization. Keep in mind that change would be about as visible at this time as the new paradigm we now ascribe to 1648 was then, but even if I'm wrong, our tendency to reify sovereignty as something subject to common understanding today is a not terribly useful exercise in fantasy. Sovereignty is what the post-modernist crowd calls a "contested discourse," and understanding that is the first step to being effective in contesting it.

Given our sovereign status---whatever that means---should Indians show up when elections are called by the colonial state? I can't say "Yes" because a more appropriate answer is "Hell, yes!" Bias out front: my first career was as a state court judge, which is an elected position. If Indians should not vote, it stands to reason they should not work for state or federal governments, especially as elected officials who have to swear an oath to "preserve, protect, and defend" the US Constitution not unlike the oath those of us who are veterans took to enter military service.

I do not understand how my citizenship in the USA or a state or a county or a city conflicts with my citizenship in an Indian nation? Without a doubt, American Indian governments sometimes have interests that do not jibe with the official policies of other political entities. How does it follow that I should not act to change those policies if such action is open to me?

The argument that one cannot serve two sovereigns is anachronistic nonsense. A sovereign is no longer a person.

To say a sovereign is dishonest, hateful, or an enemy is a statement from a time when the sovereign was a person, because these are attributes of a person. A sovereign in modern terms is a bureaucratic entity with interchangeable parts. By our citizenship, voluntary or not, we acquire the opportunity to become one of those parts or decide who does. I would argue that it's more an obligation than an opportunity, but that's just me.

Another obligation of citizenship is to serve on juries. If you shirk that obligation, what does that mean for Indians who demand jury trials?

Can you incur obligations without your consent? Everybody does. There's a sense in which you "choose" your family, your clan, your country, your land. But it's more realistic to say all these things choose you. My non-Indian friends don't understand me when I say that Europeans own land and Indians are owned by land, but that's one of many cultural disjunctions we have to work around to live together.

And we must live together. Where do you think they are going to go?

A vote is nothing more than speech, an expression of opinion, and certainly nothing less. I have opinions about whether Vladimir Putin should be head of the Russian government, and I'm happy to share those opinions. If I could vote in the Russian elections, you can bet I would, and my vote would not be based on any desire to harm Russia. Russians, of course, believe my opinions of their best interests are too trammeled by my US or Cherokee citizenships, and so they don't allow me to vote in Russia. That's their prerogative.

To put it closer to home, I would vote in both Cherokee Nation and United Keetoowah Band elections if I could. I do not think the best interests of the two conflict.

A US Supreme Court justice, dissenting in an Indian law case, wrote that great nations, like great men, should keep their word. I do not think it betrays my Cherokee citizenship if I use my voice as an involuntary US citizen to urge the US toward greatness. My very presence as an Indian in the political debate is a rebuke to the smug assertion that everything about the US is already great.

That's the view of conflicting sovereigns from the top, but the view from the bottom is more important in the daily lives of dual citizenship Indians.

In the state where I have taken up residence, we don't just elect judges. Slivers of sovereignty, the power to decide vested in the nation-state, have been delegated to other entities. The Constitution delegates power to the states and the state where I live has delegated much of that power, such that I might do little but attend to elections if the various jurisdictions did not make every effort to save money by consolidating them.

Perhaps the most important vote people cast is for school board, whether or not we have kids. Then we have the State Board of Education, which picks textbooks. If you can't see that you have an interest in the proper education of other people's kids, then maybe you should not vote.

Municipal Utility Districts. Aquifer Protection Districts. Irrelevant, I suppose, unless you drink water.

Community College Boards. Fire Protection District Boards. City Councils.

We elected a County Inspector of Hides until 2007, but I normally skipped that one because I am not a rancher, a trapper, or a tanning booth operator, and I was never sure to which it pertained. One time I did not skip it, and a friend of mine used the office as a stepping-stone to the Legislature, where he was an ally of Indians.

A vote is a written and private expression of your opinion. It differs from verbal and public expressions in that it has more impact. If you don't care to shape policy with your opinions, there are plenty of persons, human and corporate, who will be happy to do it for you.

Participation in tribal elections is less controversial, but sometimes the choices are as puzzling.

Many of us just vote for our relatives. While my living relatives are many, and one even holds high appointive office, I have not been faced with that prospect. Judging from history, voting for my relatives would not have gone well for my current opinions.

My birth namesake, Stephen Teehee, was Deputy Principal Chief in the Downing Administration, which did not reflect my views of good policy.

My great-grandfather, Henry Teehee, was a prominent Cherokee Baptist minister. The Cherokee Baptists do not reflect my views of good policy, and the reasons do not differ as between Indian and non-Indian attempts to govern by religion.

When a non-Indian starts claiming Divine authority for his or her policy preferences, hang on to your wallet.

When an Indian claims tribal tradition, do the same.

Traditions are habits and how have your habits been working out for you?

On the other hand, traditions are all that separate one tribe from another and to abandon tradition is to abandon who you are and become just another special pleading ethnic minority. I get that.

What does not follow from the necessity to protect our cultural heritage is the idea that a tribal politician needs to "think like a (insert tribe here)."

There are only two ways to think, well and poorly.

Until somebody corrects me, I can only discover three ways to know the truth and they vary in their value to government.

Truth by revelation is infallible. The problem with it is the same revelation seldom comes to all humans simultaneously. So we get Catholics and Protestants killing each other over whether it is possible to approach God directly or only through the One True Church. We get Sunni and Shi'a killing each other over who was the proper successor to the Prophet. And we get the Ghost Dance.

Truth by deduction is also infallible, but only if the major and minor premises in your deductive syllogism are correct. That is a lot harder than it sounds, and some people claim that if you reason back by deduction to First Principles, you arrive at premises that must be taken on faith. I do not think so but I firmly believe it would be a better world if every human would give that task a try.

Truth by induction is not just fallible—it's messy as all get-out. It's our understanding of inductive reasoning that leads us to respect elders. An elder has the ability to reason from the general to the specific in a more efficient way because the elder has seen more cases and watched more outcomes and learned from every one. The elder does not reinvent the cognitive wheel. The elder is the human embodiment of "practice makes perfect," but usually with sense enough not to claim perfection.

Of course, few elders want to have any truck with tribal government.

For most of us, the task of improving tribal government involves breaking patterns of behavior because few of us can claim that our current situation is working out in an optimal manner, to put it delicately. In the policy argument in Congress over expansion of the remedies available under the Indian Civil Rights

Act, it's said that one's position can be predicted by how recently one has been screwed by tribal government.

Looking around Indian Country for my entire lifetime, I see some governments getting better and some lurching from one crisis to the next.

A better test for office than traditionalism would be does the candidate participate in tribal government because of material or solidary incentives? Instead of what the candidate will give us, it is much more important to know what the candidate will ask of us.

Is the purpose of tribal government to insure the cultural survival of the tribe or to exact the greatest possible price from the colonists for killing it off?

Government for material incentives is the root of what political scientists call "the resource curse." A source of money presents itself and a government can suddenly focus on nothing beyond maximizing the gain and distributing the money to enough people to remain in power. This is general theory in political science, applicable to city, state, or tribal government.

The difference between solidary and material incentives is the difference between the casino tribes that fund the college education of every enrolled child and those that guarantee a new truck and a monthly income when a child comes of age. It's the difference between opening a new clinic or a new hotel.

What would an elder do if most elders cared about tribal government? It's hard to say, but I think it would be more than voting for relatives having jobs regardless of qualifications, for per capita payments, or to increase the power of cronies. The purpose of all government is to take care of each other in ways we cannot take care of ourselves. That purpose is not advanced by institutionalizing greed.

2 THE PRICE OF NATIONHOOD

Where you are about one half of one percent of the population, how many people can you afford to leave behind by categorical self-definition?

One obvious answer is that within your self-definition, you are one hundred percent of the population. If that self-definition is all you want, there is no problem. If you want something from the larger world, there is.

To be a "nation" is to be recognized as such in the community of nations, just as to be an Indian is to be recognized as such in an Indian community. This definition lives in what academics call "legal realism," a definition derived from how the world in fact conducts itself.

Shawnee/Lenape scholar Steven Newcomb claims the existence of tribal nationhood with a definition of "nation" from what academics call "legal formalism," a definition derived from documents treating the subject.

Neither legal realism nor legal formalism is right or wrong. They are what they are and they are useful or not for particular tasks.

From the realist or formalist perspective, there are some entities with much stronger claims to nationhood than Indian governments—Taiwan, for example—whose nationhood is problematic. Others with arguably weaker claims, such as Monaco, get away with claiming nationhood because the major powers find it convenient.

The federally recognized tribes in the US range from sophisticated governments antedating the US to some California rancherias that are nothing more than extended families squabbling over casino cash. There are also peoples for whom both language and distinctive culture are a distant memory though no fault of their own. Genocide sometimes prevails.

Too many tribal governments lack any sense of nationhood because their own people do not buy in. The reason is corruption, sometimes real and sometimes perceived, but which it is does not matter. If your own people are not willing to risk everything from their property to their lives—exactly as the founders of the US did-in defense of nationhood, then tribal government becomes like the proverbial car-chasing dog. If you catch the car, then what?

After signing the Declaration of Independence pledging "our lives, our fortunes, and our sacred honor," Ben Franklin famously stated: "We must all hang together, or assuredly we shall all hang separately." Tecumseh could have said that. The difference is that the colonists listened to Franklin and Indian nations to this day can't hear Tecumseh. Remember the inter-tribal backstabbing that came out in the Abramoff hearings?

Those of us who wish to challenge John Marshall's infamous description, "domestic, dependent nations," need to start with "dependent." Were we not reduced to dependency on purpose? Absolutely. That happened to my people three times. We are still struggling to recover from the third, the Dawes Act.

Let's say my people do recover economically. Our culture, modified to account for modernity, still lives in both Oklahoma and North Carolina. The Navajo Nation is not wealthy, but it could survive without US support and Navajo culture is strong. The Six Nations were here before the US and they are still here.

Who else? There can be good faith disagreement about which Indian nations currently have the skills to survive in shark-infested international waters, but there can be no good faith disagreement that it's a short list. How many are to be left behind?

One method of survival would be to become a client state of, say, Venezuela, or any country that has a political bone to pick with the US. Can you picture how that would work out even if the US tolerated it? Dependence is dependence. On whom is beside the point.

Steve Newcomb is absolutely correct that there is power in

9

language. The words we use frame how we think about ourselves and how others think about us. That's why it's "citizenship" rather than "membership." The primary goal of modern Indian fighters is to reduce us to race-based social clubs, less significant or autonomous than corporations or labor unions, and then to destroy us by appeal to racial neutrality, also known as white people's rights.

Aren't "citizens" connected to "nations" as members are to clubs? That would be why I envy the Canadian term "First Nations" and wonder how it came to be that Indians maintaining relations with Canada acquired that term to the exclusion of Indians who maintain relations with the US or Mexico?

"First" is a much more useful modifier than "domestic, dependent."

"Nation," unmodified and deployed industrial strength in our continuing battles with the colonial governments over self-determination, is a two-edged sword. Nationhood means responsibility and peril. Nations failing their responsibilities cease to exist. Constitutional crises, periodic sources of embarrassment in Indian Country, would potentially be fatal. If all the federally recognized tribes had independent nationhood thrust upon them tomorrow, most would fail. Some would not.

The question remains: how many are we willing to leave behind?

3 WHEN CAN WE BLAME THE VICTIMS?

Sovereignty, even in the watered down version approved by our colonial masters, carries awesome power within the tribal community. I've always been taught that power carries responsibility.

We can't sue our tribal governments in tribal court without their permission because of sovereign immunity. Of course, nobody else can sue them in any other court, either, and for the same reason.

Tribal governments wishing to attract direct foreign investment (a term here imported from international relations to Indian policy) must normally expose themselves to lawsuits over the funds invested. Newly minted tribal officials sometimes find this sinister, but it reflects the way business is normally done outside of Indian Country.

State governments and the federal government normally provide for lawsuits on contracts they enter. The federal government and all state governments have "tort claims acts" that waive sovereign immunity when the government causes damage to citizens in normal, everyday activities. You can usually sue the state if a state vehicle hits you. In most states, you can sue the state if it was negligent when it designed or repaired a public road and that negligence caused an accident.

These customary accommodations make sovereign immunity invisible and therefore tolerable to the average person doing normal things. Now and then, there is something that doesn't fit.

Famously, people have been wrongfully imprisoned for many years when newly available DNA testing proves they are innocent.

Often, the government has done nothing wrong in the innocence cases. Many are the result of confessions or eyewitness testimony, both as unreliable as they are persuasive. Every police officer who becomes a detective quickly learns that if a case is notorious enough for the front pages, it is likely to generate false confessions, so the police must always keep enough information out of the newspapers to sort though the people who want fame badly enough to claim it at the cost of their reputations. It is sad to consider yourself so inconsequential that infamy would be an improvement, but it's common.

Eyewitness identification of a stranger is difficult for anyone. When you are under stress, it becomes more difficult, and for most people being robbed or raped is highly stressful.

Cross-racial identification is even harder. Did you ever look at an Indian and try to guess the tribe? Some Indians (but few non-Indians) can. When I was in the Air Force, I was assigned to a base that trained Vietnamese, Thai, and Laotian pilots. After I was there over a year, I could give an educated guess of a pilot's nationality based on things that used to hide in my brain under "Asian."

Even in cases where the government did nothing wrong, most of us believe that somebody sent to prison for a crime they did not commit is owed some money, since they can't have their life back. Wrongful conviction would normally not be covered by a state tort claims act, but many states are passing laws that just fork over damages to innocent persons based on years lost.

Sovereign immunity means "the king can do no wrong," but most Americans believe the king can do wrong. If sovereign immunity were not full of enough holes to allow for most common claims against governments, the voters would have sunk the doctrine with a constitutional amendments by now.

Putting yourself in the shoes of a business wanting to invest with a tribal government, would you commit money without a waiver of sovereign immunity? Neither will most businesses. I have suggested that tribal governments should insert arbitration clauses that designate tribal law as the rule of decision, but that's another conversation.

There have been two cases recently where tribal citizens have lost a great deal and the nature of the public controversy has been about efforts to hold state or federal government responsible. In both cases, the tribal government was better situated to prevent the harm and ought to have had more incentive to prevent the harm.

I'm not going into the facts because the rights and wrongs of these cases do not matter to the point, which is the liberal meme of Native Americans as victims. Like the conservative meme of Indians as players of identity politics hardball. Neither idea represents us correctly.

My colleague Steve Newcomb has pointed out that we need not accept "the way things are" when things are completely irrational. Federal Indian Control Law (Robert Odawi Porter's phrase) tells us that tribal governments and individual Indians were wards of the federal government. Whether we agreed to be wards or it was thrust upon us, we need to think about that status.

Most wards grow up and become full citizens, responsible for their own decisions. The exceptions are persons suffering from physical or mental disabilities such that they will never be competent to manage their own affairs. Which kind of ward are Indian nations?

Elouise Cobell's lawsuit reminds us that the federal guardian has not been faithful to a guardian's duties, because the most basic duty is keeping track of the ward's property.

The Navajo Nation lost a lawsuit where the guardian's actions were more than merely negligent. The tribal government negotiated a lease agreement and the federal government, apparently acting in concert with the lessee, pushed the tribal government to reopen negotiations and accept less money. In over twenty years on a state court bench, I have never seen such an outrageous breach of trust.

Let us not forget, also, that some of the most horrible miscarriages of justice in federal Indian law were done "for our own good," because our childlike qualities required an adult like Uncle Sam to "protect" us.

Example A: *Lone Wolf v. Hitchcock* upheld the federal government's right to abrogate a treaty and destroy the Kiowa Reservation by allotment.

Example B: the Courts of Indian Offenses, where the ceremonies that defined our tribal identities became crimes, so we could be forced to put childish things away.

13

The recognized powers of tribal governments have been expanding ever since the colonists abandoned termination and relocation as Indian control policy. Many powers are seldom used. Few tribes issue revenue bonds, or charter corporations, or maintain a tax base independent of the U.S. Too many tribal laws ape state laws for no reason beyond convenience.

If we want to quit being wards, our governments must step up and govern. That means not just using power but being responsible to tribal citizens for bad outcomes in independent and honest tribal courts. Sovereign immunity runs against your own people only if you choose to assert it. Tribal governments should think twice about that assertion, unless they are comfortable being "wards."

There are names for the act of exercising power without responsibility, none of them complimentary.

4 THE OTHER SIDE OF TREATY ABROGATION

I could not tell if I was dreaming.

You know how it is. You wake up but something about reality doesn't seem quite right and you think you might still be asleep but you can't really tell?

I stumbled out of bed and started the coffee machine burbling and collected the newspaper from the front yard.

The sports page told me that the New Jersey Niggers had beaten the Boston Micks.

Some player on the Houston Hebes had accused the San Antonio Spics of dropping their last game to get a higher draft pick.

The league was expanding to Toronto, and since they had already honored African-Americans, Irish-Americans, Jewish-Americans and Hispanic-Americans, they wanted to name a team to honor Native Americans.

They sent out notices to all the tribal leaders, and they told us we could have whatever we wanted: Prairie Niggers, if the New Jersey team did not object, Redskins, Savages, Warriors, Heathens, Braves, Bucks--and of course the cheerleaders would be the Squaws, unless we wanted to modernize the language and just call them the Cunts.

But the tribal leaders voted for a write-in candidate, the Treaties.

"Toronto Treaties." It has a nice ring to it.

But the league was puzzled. What kind of a name is that?

"If the United States and Canada want to honor the First Nations," said the tribal leaders, "honor our treaties."

And there was a sidebar story. It seems that the President of the United States and the Prime Minister of Canada had heard this and called a joint press conference.

"We had no idea," they said, "that our countries have violated so many agreements with Native Americans. We have formed a joint commission to recommend how to make it up to the survivors, and we have each proposed legislation tendering a formal apology."

And it was at that moment I knew I was dreaming.

Since my beloved Cherokee Nation has determined to abrogate a treaty with the United States, that dream has turned into a very scary nightmare. One of the favorite pastimes of Indian lawyers has always been disputing among themselves which US Supreme Court decisions are the worst of the worst for the interests of Indians. Walter Echo-Hawk recently wrote a book on his picks. I make some picks in a chapter of my tribal policy book, *Sequoyah Rising*.

Two cases are often the scum rising to the top in this melting pot of ugliness.

Lone Wolf v. Hitchcock, holding that the US can abrogate treaties with the Indian nations based on a finding that abrogation is in our best interests.

Cherokee Nation v. Georgia, holding that we cannot bring original actions in the Supreme Court for treaty violations the way other nations can.

This backdrop of bad faith is the barb inside the famous words of Hugo Black that Indian lawyers call the all-purpose federal Indian law dissent: "Great Nations, like great men, should keep their word."

The most potent political weapons in our arsenal have always been our treaties. For the most part, we kept our word and the United States did not. The Cherokee Supreme Court's decision on the citizenship of the freedmen states flatly that we have not abrogated the treaty between the United States and the Cherokee Nation in 1866 containing the declaration that all "free colored persons" living in the Cherokee Nation or who returned within six months "shall have all the rights of native Cherokees."

The opinion neglects to tell us why this is not so, assuming it self-evident that we can stand outside history and separate the rights of citizenship from citizenship because it's to our advantage almost 150 years later.

At the time, why did the United States care? Because the Cherokee slaves would otherwise be the responsibility of the Freedmen's Bureaus.

Why did the Cherokee Nation not care? Because we had already freed the slaves as a matter of Cherokee law before the treaty was negotiated, and our "intruder problem" was white people taking our property (among other crimes) and hiding behind federal jurisdiction. What we wanted was respect for Cherokee law, and it was white people avoiding Cherokee law, not black people.

Didn't the Cherokee people vote to abrogate the treaty? No, they did not, in two senses.

First, the disenrollment of the freedmen was purposely presented at a special election rather than a general election to drastically limit the turnout to those who perceived they had a dog in the fight. Racial prejudice runs deep in rural Oklahoma, where *Brown v. Board of Education* was considered an unwarranted imposition of federal power.

Second, the same tribal leaders who squirm over the threatened cutoff of federal funds assured the voters that a treaty was not being abrogated. The voters cannot be accused of approving something they were specifically told was not at issue.

Then there is the argument that the treaty was invalid in the first place because it ended the hostilities in the Civil War, where the Cherokee fought on the losing side (which is not exactly to say that we lost, as Stand Watie was the last Confederate general to surrender).

This is simply nonsense, because treaties end most wars and the winner always has the whip hand.

A really dangerous argument thrown into the debate is known in lawyer Latin as *tu quoque*, "you do it, too." That is, the treaty was already dead because the US had violated it in some respects.

Whether the treaty obligation exists now in light of changed circumstances is a valid question, and one that must be parsed carefully in the law of treaty abrogation, but no such parsing ever took place in any of the three branches of Cherokee government. There has only been denial and obfuscation.

In *Lone Wolf v. Hitchcock*, the US Supreme Court decided, essentially, that Secretary Ethan Hitchcock would be empowered to act in the best interests of the Kiowa over the expressions of that interest by the Kiowa Principal Chief. In history's rear view mirror, we know that Chief Lone Wolf was right, but had Lone Wolf been wrong do a sovereign people not have a right to proceed to Hell in their own chosen hand basket?

We know now and have known since the day it was decided that the *Lone Wolf* case was an outrageous expansion of the reasons for treaty abrogation recognized in law. Because Indian nations have not been in the habit of abrogating treaties, we have no statement by an Indian court of in what respect *Lone Wolf* was wrong and therefore what the rules ought to be. This is the opportunity the Cherokee Supreme Court declined by adopting the farcical position of the Cherokee executive rather than reaching the same result, if it must, in the manner of a court.

The interruption in federal funds to the Cherokee, some say, was a result of meddling by the Congressional Black Caucus rather than the normal enforcement of federal anti-discrimination rules. It might more profitably bring to mind the negotiating posture of a federal treaty commissioner quoted in *South Dakota v. Yankton Sioux Tribe*:

> *"I want you to understand that you are absolutely dependent upon the Great Father to-day for a living. Let the Government send out instructions to your agent to cease to issue these rations, let the Government instruct your agent to cease to issue your clothes. . . . Let the Government instruct him to cease to issue your supplies, let him take away the money to run your schools with, and I want to know what you would do. Everything you are wearing and eating is gratuity. Take all this away and throw this people wholly upon their own responsibility to take care of themselves, and what would be the result? Not one-fourth of your people could live through the winter, and when the grass grows again it would be nourished by the dust of all the balance of your noble tribe."*

As a Cherokee citizen, I hope we are not in such a fix in the 21st century. Treaty abrogation is a sovereign right but it comes with a hefty price tag if you are dependent.

Remember the position of the modern Indian fighters: every program that benefits Indians, all of Title 25 of the US Code, is racial discrimination against white people. Our response to that is the distinction between "race" and citizenship that the Cherokee Supreme Court has trashed without analysis. This distinction is what has kept money flowing to Indian country over the objections of the Indian fighters.

The danger is obvious that the Congressional Indian fighters could use the Cherokee case as a wedge against all appropriations to tribes, even those required by treaty. Circumstances have changed, you see, and "race discrimination" cannot be tolerated.

A final and much less obvious danger lurks in simply accepting the death of Indian treaties, which does not, with all respect to Hamlet, represent for Indians "a consummation devoutly to be wish'd."

Congress ended Indian treaty making in 1871 by a legislative rider. It's not clear that Congress had the power to do that or, if Congress did, that it could be done with a rider. Negotiating treaties is a quintessential executive function.

The Senate (alone) could refuse to ratify a treaty with an Indian nation, but it's not clear that Congress could stop the negotiation of one. With the right President, some of the most galling infringements on our sovereignty by the courts could be attacked around the reach of the Indian fighters in the House of Representatives. This might be yet another reason for an Indian nation not to act recklessly in abrogating a treaty.

Or I might, once again, be dreaming.

5 THE RIGHTS OF GAIA

In the ironically named *Citizens United* case, the US Supreme Court followed the logic of a line of cases declaring corporations to be "persons" within the meaning of the Fourteenth Amendment and found them equal to human beings in the matter of spending money to influence politics. Willard Mitt Romney, in his run for President, later kicked it up a notch by declaring in answer to a hostile taxation question at the Iowa State Fair, "Corporations are people, my friend."

I'm a mere retired judge, but my own view is that corporations are legal technology, ink on paper, and they have no rights not conferred on them by the legislature. I would go farther and urge tribal governments to enact business codes that limit corporate activities and require a tribal charter to do business on tribal land. But that's just me

In keeping with my personal tradition of finding odd connections in the news, I see that the indigenous President of Bolivia, Evo Morales, is about to promulgate *la Ley de Derechos de la Madre Tierra*. In English, "the law of the rights of Mother Earth."

Morales did not pull this out of his sombrero; the idea of humans as one small part of an interconnected universe is common to many indigenous traditions, including my own. It's the difference between asking pardon of an animal if you take its life or believing humans are deputized by God to cut any swath through the natural world that they find convenient.

Moving from spirituality to science, the indigenous worldview finds

20

expression in the Gaia hypothesis of James Lovelock and Lynn Margulis, holding that all animals (including humans) and all plants and even inorganic materials are part of one incredibly complex system that has a preferred homeostasis. That homeostasis is optimal for the currently existing life, and the hypothesis holds that Gaia will adjust her systems to maintain it.

That's a very optimistic idea. Let's hope it pans out.

Completing the circle back to Morales' new law, we have Justice William O. Douglas' 1972 dissenting opinion in *Sierra Club v. Morton*, an opinion that generated as much vitriol against Justice Douglas as any he ever penned, and that's a tough competition. I've heard it cited as evidence that the old man had stayed on the Court too long and his reasoning power had faded.

The Sierra Club had brought a lawsuit to prevent logging of the Mineral King Valley, a land aboriginally occupied by the Yokut people. The Sierra Club's concern was encroachment upon Sequoia National Park.

Who "owns" Sequoia National Park? All citizens of the United States. Therefore, the Supreme Court reasoned, the Sierra Club had no "standing" to bring a lawsuit. If the Sierra Club had standing, the argument went, anybody has standing, and nothing can ever get done because of all the lawsuits.

This theory of standing legalizes an ecological theory proposed by Garrett Hardin. He described the problem of numerous people sharing a resource and therefore an interest in not depleting the resource. However, each individual—consulting only his rational self-interest—takes amounts of the common resource such that the resource is in fact depleted. This is why governments make hunting and fishing seasons, bag limits, and sometimes ban the taking of juveniles or females. It's why if you want to take an elk on the Jicarilla Apache Reservation, you will get in line for a permit.

The short version is that if we all "own" it then nobody owns it and so nobody will take care of it and we will all lose it. "It" might be timber, clean water, or game. Anything that can be depleted.

I am reminded of a report on the depletion of fisheries in the Northeast, where a number of fishers were asked: if they could make a 15% annual return on their investment forever or a 60% return and the fish would be gone in ten years, which would they choose? Invariably, the fishers who were descended from fishermen chose sustainable harvest, while those who had a trawler as a new investment were more inclined to cash out. This, along with the histories of many Indian nations, suggests that "the tragedy of the commons" has a strong cultural component.

In the *Sierra Club* case, the Supreme Court institutionalized the tragedy of the commons by holding that nobody outside government can stand up and prevent a collective blunder. Everybody knows government is always a rational actor, right? Especially when corporations can make campaign contributions just like other people.

In dissent, Justice Douglas located the legal standing not in the Sierra Club but in the trees themselves, and earned himself decades of ridicule. Douglas claimed the only proper question was whether the Sierra Club had the resources and the motive to actually represent the interests of the trees,

Douglas did not limit this idea to living things. Had his dissent been law, some of us here in Texas would have been able to file a lawsuit some years ago when there was a proposal to allow Enchanted Rock, which I've been told is sacred to the Tonkawa and Comanche peoples, to be cut up and hauled off for building materials.

Thanks to Evo Morales, Justice Douglas' dissent is about to become law in Bolivia. I cannot resist pointing out that in our country, corporations are persons but Mother Earth is not.

6 MANAGE VICE OR VICE MANAGES US

First, let's be clear what I mean by "vice." That would be money made off your bad habits, as opposed to my own bad habits. Your bad habits are immoral; mine are endearing eccentricities.

Vice is a culture-bound idea, and individuals within cultures have different tolerances. To some, any drinking is a vice. To others, any drunkenness. Still, any lawyer who has picked a jury in a DWI case knows that there are people who do not consider even drunken driving to be wrong.

I personally quit smoking dope in the US when I took the oath to be a judge, not because I think it's wrong but because I cannot deal with the hypocrisy, which raised the social cost of getting high over what I was willing to accept. Mileage differs for other judges, I'm sure.

Judges are just people, people. So are police officers.

In the past few years, I have seen the destruction of a Texas-Mexico borderlands culture I have always loved. Like most bad effects from drugs, it is the prohibition rather than the drugs causing the destruction.

When I was consulting Prof. Google about Mexico, I was shocked that a number of travel sites take the line that "you are perfectly safe as long as you are not involved in drugs."

That's nonsense, and it's dangerous nonsense. I started paying attention years ago when thirty *gringos* died of gunshots in one year in Nuevo Laredo. As far as I could tell, none of them was doing more than loitering at the corner of flesh and bullet while shopping or eating.

Since then, the Cadillac Bar, which claimed to have invented the margarita, went out of business.

In 2009, some of my students from Indiana University took one of those inexpensive "Spring Break in Cancun" packages. Every one of them was the victim of crime. Separate crimes, except one group mugging.

The guys who used to truck arts and crafts from the interior to the *Mercado Central* are out of business. Nobody will risk death to buy *hueraches* from Oaxaca or tile from Saltillo or coffee beans from Chiapas or even a cheap bottle of tequila.

The *barbacoa* joints on the main drag where I used to sit and eat tortillas and beans when I had no money are out of business.

The guys they called the Green Angels who patrolled the highways between the border and the major cities below are all out of work. Motorists travel, when they do, in high-speed convoys that stop for nothing.

The granny who used to roast *pepitos* on the *Plaza Mayor* in Reynosa has lost that income. The shoeshine boys now run dope, I presume, because there are few shoes to shine. A friend who lives near Ciudad Acuña sent me a photo he took on a Friday afternoon. It was sad and shocking to see nobody on the street at that hour.

I grew up with the Texas and Mexico economies tying the countries together like shoelaces. The legitimate part of it is all gone. Even most of the whorehouses are closed. The *farmacias* where you got your antibiotics over the counter are closed--you don't think the Mexican customers kept that many *farmacias* going, do you? Those wonderful farmers' markets where you could get avocados or limes or mangoes by the case are shrunken to the size of grocery stores. Mexican vanilla seldom shows up on this side of the border anymore.

In those days, it took no credential to enter Mexico in the border zone and only a "tourist card" available at any Mexican consulate for longer stays in the interior. Coming back was a matter of convincing the border guard of your citizenship. When interrogated, I used to say "Cherokee Nation," and the only time that did not get me right in I had to answer some questions about the geography of Oklahoma that any Okie could answer. If I claimed "Cherokee Nation" since September 11, 2001, that would probably get me at least a body cavity search from Bubba of the Border Patrol.

A passport is now required, and one of my students who got hers stolen in Cancun had to go to Mexico City so the US Embassy could handle getting her home. Apparently, since 9-11, a college kid without a passport is too big a deal for a mere consulate to handle.

Fast money income on the border is now drugs and guns (in opposite directions), robbery, and kidnapping. The American stores that used to cater to Mexican shoppers for small appliances are hurting.

As much as I despise bullfighting, I have to observe you don't see those big colorful posters anymore advertising some dude in tight trousers on tour from Spain.

The guys who used to do car customizing on the cheap now do nothing but alter vehicles for smuggling. I say bring back the velour and the fuzzy dice! Even if you don't want to be a lowrider, you have to admit it's harmless fun and it has been a lot of legitimate economic activity...back when we could cruise unarmed.

Look at what we've lost! Look at what Mexico has lost! I want it all back. The *barbacoa*, the whores, the drunken tourists and even the barbaric bullfights. My world is smaller and I don't like the shrinking of my world one bit.

All of this so we can fight our futile "war on drugs" and maintain the right of one cowboy to walk into a gun shop and buy a hundred rifles....because maybe he has a big family?

Making Americans go though more changes to buy guns in big lots does not threaten our sacred right as individuals to go about armed to the teeth.

Legalizing drugs as a matter of law or of enforcement policy has never caused huge and permanent spikes in drug use but rather small and temporary ones. Are Americans that different? There will always be junkies no matter what the law is. Tax the dope to treat the junkies. Take away the need to steal to get drugs of dubious quality. Hit the drug cartels the only place they have feelings, in their Swiss bank accounts. Did we learn nothing from alcohol prohibition?

I want my borderlands back!

I remember shortly after I was elected to the Travis County Court at Law, one of three judges hearing criminal cases, we asked for two new courts. It was a reasonable request, but it was obvious to me at the time that if all criminal cases related to alcohol were subtracted, we had plenty of judges.

Many of us forget that alcohol prohibition was a progressive idea with which some Christian fundamentalists happened to agree. Hearing criminal cases, I came to understand why, and if it were not for the bad economic consequences I could support alcohol prohibition in spite of my liking for frozen margaritas.

I wonder if this country learned nothing from alcohol prohibition because the "war on drugs" is no different.

Want a running dipstick on how the local drug war is going? Forget amounts seized or dealers sentenced.

Give one teenager in each school district $100 and tell him or her to bring you as much methamphetamine, cocaine, or heroin as that sum will buy. Without opening the baggie of white powdery substance you will get in return, send it off to the crime lab. You want to know three things.

Is it the real deal? How much by volume did $100 buy? What level of purity? When a controlled substance goes up in price, the product gets "stepped on" more before reaching the retail user.

Enter all this into your computer every month for a year, do a little combination of bar graph and color code, and you will have a picture of your drug war at any given time, immune from press releases about the "street value" of seizures.

In some neighborhoods, I expect you could produce an algorithm to express the price of addictive drugs in the burglary rate, but direct measures are superior to both indirect measures and self-interested propaganda. What you need to know is price action.

Radical changes in the price line are to be avoided. Too low produces overdose danger from competition over purity. Too high produces more burglaries or even robberies.

People do not quit when the monetary price goes up. They quit when the social price exacted by family and friends gets too high or the user has a life-changing health crisis. As a sentencing judge, I think my job is to use the limited tools the law presents to raise the social costs of using. The magic of "drug courts" is that they give judges who understand what is going on more tools to raise the cost to the individual without raising the cost to the public.

Like judges, the police are politically limited in how much

truth they can reveal, but I should say that using kids to keep tabs on drug prices is no slap at law enforcement. Vice has to be easily available to the public, like any business.

I presume most voters would prioritize vice somewhat below violent crime and property crime. To say that a beat officer knows who is hooking or dealing drugs is not a valid criticism of the police. Read a few hundred warrant applications and you will understand that it's necessary to get information from people who have it.

When there is police corruption, it invariably starts in the vice squad, where the duty is to stop behavior that can't be stopped serviced by individuals who may make more money in one transaction than a policeman makes in a year. The management perspective is that you don't let people stay in vice too long. On the other hand, vice cops need to know the players and that takes time.

Kids know where to buy drugs. Tourists can quickly engage prostitutes. These businesses must be visible enough for customers but not too visible for the comfort level of the community. The police have to act when people get angry.

When people are not angry, corrupt police are paid off with money and honest police are paid off with information, often in cases where there is a dire need for information. Austin police, in my time, were honest. When they did something wrong, it was overzealousness rather than trying to retire above their pay grade.

With all the evils that flow from prohibition, I still don't buy the "victimless crime" argument, and destroying it was one of the goals of my teaching. The "victimless" issue is simply whether the government owns the power to prohibit self-destructive conduct, and this is not a serious question in the current state of our law. The fact issue of dangerousness if for the legislatures, not the courts.

The two principal limits on governmental power are due process and equal protection. Those limits have not been applied to vice crimes and it's hard to see how to apply them coherently.

There is no question that the government owns the power to prevent you from doing harm to yourself, and that there are valid arguments about how the cost/benefit analysis should come down in regulation of alcohol and drugs. Less so in prostitution and gambling and my favorite personal vice, enchiladas.

All that admitted, the destruction of the Texas-Mexico borderlands culture is an extraterritorial result of enforcement by the fantasy that it's possible to stamp out other people's vices by diverting law into what is a social and medical enterprise. History will not judge this kindly. Will Indian nations, many still practicing alcohol prohibition, absorb history's judgment?

7 A TORT IS NOT AN ENGLISH MUFFIN

American Indians understand living in a web of relationships that carry privileges and impose duties. Therefore, I wonder, why is tort law virtually absent in the routine of tribal governance?

Tort law in the dominant culture normally does not come from statutes but from the English Common Law as it has branched off from England to 49 states, all but Louisiana.

In most states, we carry around a free-floating duty not to be "negligent." This is nothing complicated. It means that we should act as a reasonable person would act in the same or similar circumstances. If we fail this duty, we owe anybody we harm.

What we owe could be complicated. Most people agree on medical bills and lost wages, called "special damages."

We begin to disagree on "general damages," packed into phrases like "pain and suffering" and "mental anguish." It's easy to pooh-pooh the idea of general damages if you don't think about some obvious questions.

What is a tiny child's life worth?

What sum of money would you take to suffer what you have suffered since your injury?

After the medical bills are paid, what is it worth to you to lose an eye or an ear or a testicle? What are you whining about? You have two of them, right?

General damages account for needing a lawyer to make your claim but having no money. We solve this with "contingent fees," meaning that the lawyer does not get paid unless she wins and what

29

she gets paid is a percentage of the damages. Therefore, if the damages are limited to medical bills and lost wages, the injured person could never break even.

Complications in the Common Law grow for honest reasons. At first, the rule was that if the injured party was also negligent, he recovered nothing. There was a famous case involving the duty of an employer to provide a safe working environment. The employee was negligent because he had been drinking. He was injured because the roof fell on him, but he recovered nothing because he had been drinking.

Why, you may well ask, don't we just ask a court to apply common sense to each case? Because judges are easily captured by repeat players in the system. The major repeat players in a tort system are insurance companies.

Why not leave the hard questions to juries? We do that. Sometimes it works. Sometimes we get results like an individual in Texas who was severely injured in an accident she did not cause, but the insurance company's lawyer managed to get in front of the jury that she had been a political candidate of the Socialist Workers Party. For that reason, she got nothing.

English Common Law is nothing but a set of tribal customs that started getting written down by an especially powerful tribe in the year 1066, as white people reckon time. There is no reason why those tribal customs are inherently superior to any other tribe's customs, but they may be superior in particular ways. This is because the situations to which the customs respond are universal. People interact and people get hurt, always, and most people agree that it's not fair to make innocent people bear the burden of their injuries alone.

Social duty is on the clearest level in homicide, the taking of a human life. The English looked down on some Indian justice systems, my own included, because to us all such losses were the same and a life demanded a life in return unless the relatives agreed to settle for something less.

To the English, and to most justice systems today, a homicide has different ramifications depending on whether the death was intentional, reckless, or merely the result of negligence--in other words, an accident.

Even when homicide is a crime, it is still a tort, as are robbery, rape, assault—most intentional crimes contain a tort. Criminals usually don't get sued because they have no money. In some states, the government compensates crime victims, on the theory that the government has failed to protect them.

It comes to my mind that when the Supreme Court took away the jurisdiction of tribal courts to punish non-Indians for crimes on Indian land in *Oliphant v. Suquamish Indian Tribe*, it said nothing about torts. Even when a tort judgment cannot be collected in full, there are ways to make the life of a judgment debtor miserable with repeated post-judgment discovery demands and turnover orders and liens.

Judgment creditors have a great deal of power to track every dime a judgment debtor makes to the point where a judgment debtor has time for little but responding to court orders to produce this or that information. Failure to produce the information means going to jail not for debt, but for contempt of the court order to produce information

The debtor produces the information and gets out of jail...and the process starts over again.

Handled smartly, a tribal tort system could encourage non-Indians who harm Indians on Indian land to, in the immortal term coined by Willard Mitt Romney, "self-deportation."

This is the challenge of Indian tribal governments: to govern, and to resolve these universal problems in ways both objectively fair and predictable. When tribal law conquers that challenge, the opinions of dead Englishmen do not matter. When tribal law fails, the opinions of live Indians do.

Sometimes, a failure to act is negligence.

8 INDIANS AND DIVERSITY

At this writing, the Supreme Court has just heard a case about affirmative action in university admissions, where my alma mater is on the side of diversity for a change. Most observers agree diversity is likely to lose, but if that happens it does not mean Indians have to quit banging on the doors of higher education.

Indians know diversity, and knew it before Columbus got lost. My people, woodland hunters and farmers, traded with salt water fishermen on the coast and some copper ornaments smelted in Cherokee country turned up in Southwestern pueblos, where they grew the Three Sisters crops on dry land farms and built with stucco. When the Spanish proved unable to keep track of their livestock, many tribes took up the buffalo culture on the Great Plains. Athabascan speakers live in icy Alaska and desert Utah. We know diversity.

To the colonists, we are all "Indians," one of the most exotic minorities in modern politics. We all have this experience at some point if we leave home: "Do you want to be called Indian or Native American?" Tribal identity requires explanation, and it does get tiresome.

African-Americans, by the tragedy they have endured, bigfoot any discussion of diversity in the United States. The Civil War was, much as the Confederates denied it afterwards, about slavery.

The Civil War added the 14th Amendment to the Constitution, importing into law the statement of faith in the Declaration of Independence that "all men are created equal."

Republicans, then the anti-slavery party, controlled the Congress and the Presidency, but the Supreme Court changes much more slowly and it remained in the hands of Democrats. The Democratic Court quickly sliced and diced the 14th Amendment, gutting the Privileges and Immunities Clause in *The Slaughterhouse Cases* (1873) and eviscerating the Equal Protection Clause in *Plessy v. Ferguson* (1896). Legal equality died for another half century.

Homer Plessy's case was particularly ironic. Plessy was one-eighth African-American by blood quantum, and so considered himself a white man—but the Court found he was not white enough to sit where he pleased on public transportation. There things stood until Rosa Parks came along not claiming to be a white woman, but insisting she was a human being.

The fight to pry education loose from "separate but equal" started at the graduate level, where facilities were too scarce to be made equal. Texas was sued in the seminal law school case, *Sweatt v. Painter*, a case that began in the courthouse where I spent my first career. The first thing the state court did was give Texas time to create a "Negro Law School." This law school was staffed by practicing black lawyers, not the widely published scholars found at any top law school like the University of Texas.

In 1950, the Supreme Court cut though this transparent nonsense. On any level, schools are not "equal," and the Justices on the Supreme Court, graduates of excellent law schools, knew that. It would be satisfying to end this by pointing out that the state courthouse where Sweatt vainly sought justice was renamed in 2005 "The Heman Marion Sweatt Travis County Courthouse," but the fight for equality goes on, as does Texas' role in it.

The "separate but equal" fiction finally died as a matter of

law in the famous 1954 case, *Brown v. Board of Education*.
Prevailing counsel in that case was Thurgood Marshall, who
himself had been denied admission to the University of
Maryland School of Law on account of his race. Later, President
Lyndon Johnson appointed Marshall to the Supreme Court and
today the University of Maryland Law Library is named after
Marshall, the man not good enough to study there.

Brown killed segregation as a matter of law, but housing
patterns continued segregation as a matter of fact. For a few
years, there were attempts to achieve racial integration by
having kids ride school buses, but that turned into a cultural
wedge issue and was eventually beaten back. I personally
bought a house in a racially integrated neighborhood in Austin
both because I favored integration and because I would rather
my son be able to walk to school.

As the Harvard Civil Rights Project has documented,
schools in the United States have been re-segregating since
1988. It should be no surprise that predominantly minority
schools lag in per pupil spending, teacher salaries, and results,
whether measured by test scores or by college admission rates.
The race that experiences the most going to school with
children of the same color is…the "white" race.

That's diversity in K-12. It takes little imagination to see
how segregating whites in K-12 leads to mostly white
universities. For reasons I shall explain, Indians are better fixed
to push into those white universities than other minorities, no
matter how *Fisher v. University of Texas* is decided.

All racial discourse has been nonsensical since we've
understood *H. sapiens* as one species with common ancestors.
"White" is about color, and there are more differences among
whites than there are between whites and other "races."
"Indian," all Indians know, simply refers to persons indigenous
to the Americas, and the only time we have more similarities
than differences is when we are attacked for being Indian.

The demand that our children be exposed to a first rate
education is not nonsensical, and that demand has the mud of
racial discourse all over it. For Indians, however, there may be a

way to press that demand outside of racial fantasies, at least on the college level. To say why, it becomes necessary to get out into the weeds of affirmative action law.

Those who wish to make the phrase "affirmative action" distasteful need to understand its origins, but not nearly so much as those of us who wish to defend it. When the newly elected President John F. Kennedy inquired about racial discrimination in federal employment, he met the refrain that there were "no qualified Negroes." The result was Executive Order 10925, requiring the government to take "affirmative action" to find qualified applicants.

Subsequently, the term "affirmative action" found its way into the regulations implementing Title VII of the Civil Rights Act of 1964, which banned all discrimination in hiring by businesses involved in interstate commerce, excepting tribal employers. Is it fair that an Indian can sue a white employer for race discrimination but a white person can't sue a tribal employer for the same thing? Yes, for reasons I hope to make clear.

As a result of generations of inferior education, or because of racial differences in intelligence—depending on your point of view—whites continued to dominate higher education even after overt racial exclusion was struck down. Some colleges then undertook "affirmative action" to diversify their student bodies.

Inevitably, a rejected white student filed suit alleging racial discrimination in college admissions. Federal courts had no problem recognizing that so-called reverse discrimination is unlawful but that institutions with a history of racial exclusion could consider race in admissions as a remedy for past discrimination.

Leaving aside how that logic stinks of "corruption of blood," punishing children for the sins of parents, the effects of past discrimination get harder to prove over time. In 1978, the Court in *University of California Regents v. Baake* deadlocked over whether considering race as a "plus factor" in medical school admission was a remedy for past discrimination. The swing vote, Justice Lewis Powell, offered an alternative rationale: "diversity."

My university teaching was performed at one very diverse school and one less so. I'm here to tell you Justice Powell was onto something. What the affirmative action critics do not understand is that diverse voices in the classroom are a benefit principally to the white majority. The benefit to minority individuals who earn more over time and are able to offer their children similar opportunities is not insignificant, but the immediate results in terms of the classroom experience are easier to see.

After *Baake*, any notion of "racial quotas" was dead but the goal of diversity as an educational value was very much alive. I thought at the time that the drawback of "remedy for past discrimination" was that it would end in a generation, while the value of teaching in a diverse environment will outlive even the idiotic fiction of "race."

So I thought until 2003, when the Supreme Court took up a pair of cases challenging affirmative action admissions at the University of Michigan. In *Grutter v. Bollinger*, the Court both adopted the diversity rationale and set a time limit of 25 years on using it. As a teacher, I find this preposterous, but as a lawyer, I smell a compromise in that time limit.

If such an illogical compromise was necessary to uphold the diversity rationale in 2003, the chances that a more conservative Court will continue to recognize diversity as a value almost ten years later are not good.

This is a tragedy for education, but the impact on Indians can be limited by tribal governments willing to go to bat for access to universities. This is legal because a preference for educated Indians is not about "race." It's about tribal citizenship. Neither is Indian hiring preference by tribal governments about race, but rather about a dire necessity every government faces to see its citizens employed.

Every time a tribal government has to enter negotiations with a state government over anything, Indian set-asides in college admissions could and should be on the table. You want a cut of casino money? You want your law enforcement officers deputized on our land? You want an easement over our land? Educate our kids.

This does not solve the problem, because the root of it is inferior K-12 schools that do not produce test scores that are competitive in the regular admissions process. An even more robust predictor of test scores than per pupil expenditures is parental involvement in the process. This is how lack of education becomes hereditary.

Whoa, what's the big deal about test scores? Aren't they culturally biased? No doubt. So is education generally. That's why the scores correlate with college grades. No point in getting our kids in if they cannot do the work. Tribal governments and Indian parents have to work the problem from both ends.

My mail tells me that Indians, like most Americans, are conflicted about affirmative action, but have little idea what it means. I have written about where it came from but not defined it. The time to engage that task is here.

The practice of affirmative action has two aspects, net broadening and preferences. Net broadening refers to fishing where the fish are: historically black colleges, Hispanic serving colleges, tribal colleges. Net broadening has been sufficient to enroll plenty of women and Asians, because those groups have the test scores to walk though the front door. Their underrepresentation was a straightforward artifact of discrimination in recruiting and admissions.

While the underrepresentation of Indians, blacks, and Hispanics comes partially from overt discrimination, they also suffer from systemic discrimination by inferior education in K-12 schools, aggravated by generations of low expectations by both schools and parents. These people are like white kids from rural Appalachia, products of similarly inferior schools and low expectations, but the racists use the disparity in test scores to argue that we are naturally suited to take orders and they are naturally suited to give orders.

One big obstacle for first generation college students is the myth that all colleges are alike. I could easily have succumbed to that myth if I had not served in the military with people who were not first generation college students. The most educated person in my family was an aunt who was a registered nurse, but her entire experience was focused on the certification. Vocational education is important, but it's not the subject here. Anyone can get into some college, somewhere, now that overt discrimination is illegal. Once in, if you are looking for technical certification in anything from computer systems to respiratory therapy, you can acquire your certification and if you were born to a family of manual laborers, as I was, your life will be entirely different from the lives of your parents. Good for you, but you don't need affirmative action.

So we come to the other prong of affirmative action, preferences, which the naysayers would claim is all of affirmative action. The antis also overlook the rule that only if two candidates are equally qualified, affirmative action gives the nod to a member of an underrepresented class.

We who are in favor of affirmative action often overlook that if you give a bureaucrat the choice of a decision they have to justify (pick the white person) or a decision they do not have to justify (pick the minority), the result will be less qualified rather than equally qualified minorities getting preference. The predictable social outcome is the stigma on "affirmative action babies," like Supreme Court Justice Clarence Thomas, who without affirmative action would have gotten no closer to Yale Law School than working in the cafeteria. Now, he is likely to be a decisive vote in striking down affirmative action.

To avoid the stigma, the only time I mentioned my tribe in college was to request a press release to the tribal paper when I graduated. I benefitted from the impulse behind affirmative action anyway, because I could not hide rural poverty and lack of a high school diploma. I, too, could never have been accepted at Yale Law without affirmative action, but I got waitlisted and declined to wait.

I learned the hard way that there is no avoiding the stigma. As long as affirmative action exists, people will assume minorities with degrees got an extra hand. To have the policy, the price is worth paying.

I've now spent fifteen years doing my best to help first generation college students, many minorities and many not. George W. Bush graduated from a fine prep school and then skated though Yale with C's. He was then admitted to Harvard Business School. My kids (biological or professional mentees) could never do that.

If I had told Yale I'm Cherokee, I expect I would have been admitted straight up rather than waitlisted. However, I had graduated from a top shelf state university *magna cum laude* and I had a decent LSAT score. At Yale, I would have been like Clarence Thomas, occupying a seat for which a white person with higher test scores was turned down. If the elite schools depended exclusively on test scores, they would be virtually all white and Asian.

Elite schools have better sense than to admit people who can't do the work. They have to cater to American royalty, but it's in everybody's best interests that they also serve the value of social mobility, and that elite school admission practices cause American royalty to rub elbows with the *hoi polloi*.

We who have no family to guide us can look up at the elite universities, the fruit we have been taught not to expect, and say it's probably sour anyway. Or we can shake the damn tree.

9 THE FERENGI CLAN OF THE WANABI NATION

Forrest Carter, Carlos Castaneda, Ward Churchill, Iron Eyes Cody, Jamake HIghwater, Nasdijj, Princess Pale Moon, Andrea and Justine Smith, Mary Thunder, Dhyani Ywahoo.

Some of these people have done good work; others have profited only themselves. Some have traded in valuable insights; others in execrable garbage. They have one thing in common.

A question litigated in the Massachusetts Senate race in 2012 was whether Sen. Elizabeth Warren belongs on that list. I am personally unclear about the standards of admission, so I will be thinking out loud. I contributed to Elizabeth Warren's campaign before and after her opponent nominated her for inclusion, so feel free to consider these remarks biased for that reason.

Nobody likes to be taken in, but I have not been. I contributed because I believe Elizabeth Warren holds promise to be the most effective representative of the 99% to serve in Congress in my generation. But if she has traded on a fake Indian identity, I certainly would think less of her.

I'm puzzled by the way the question has been addressed, and Ms. Warren did not help with her imbecilic remarks about "high cheekbones." As in the cases of Ward Churchill and Andrea Smith, the most common way of looking at the question is genealogy, the quest for a Cherokee in the woodpile, as it were. Pray tell, in what sense is somebody Indian if they have to hire a genealogist to prove it?

I was born and raised in the Creek Nation, and some of our customs are remarkably similar. We share the history of removal to Indian Territory and the violation of our treaties to create the State of Oklahoma. We produced the most effective organizers against the Dawes Act abomination in the Cherokee Redbird Smith and the Creek Chitto Harjo. But I never, ever, thought I was the same as a Creek. Different language, different stories, different traditions of governing—let's face it, different peoples.

How can you maintain a tribal identity without knowing at least some of what that identity means?

A genealogist in Boston claimed to have discovered that Elizabeth Warren's g-g-g-grandmother is listed on a marriage application as Cherokee. This would not tell us blood quantum because, even in those times, one was either a Cherokee citizen or not.

Elizabeth Warren's alleged Cherokee ancestor would have been a contemporary of John Ross, Cooweescowee, the Bird Clan Cherokee who led the tribal government though our most tragic confrontations with American greed. Ross was 1/8 Cherokee by blood, as I am. I draw the conclusion that if Warren's ancestor were in fact Cherokee, we would still know nothing about her blood quantum.

A prominent Cherokee scholar, Dr. Richard Allen, points out that Warren's ancestor was allegedly married to a white man in Tennessee at a time when such a marriage would have been prohibited by anti-miscegenation laws. Those laws only fell when struck down by the Supreme Court in 1967, a blow for equality every bit as significant as the legalization of gay marriage in our time. Like the prohibitions on gay marriage, anti-miscegenation laws were justified by a comical admixture of fake science and superstition, only comical to those not separated from persons they loved.

It's only fair to admit the Cherokee Nation had such laws as well, but applying only to "Negroes." However, white Cherokee citizens were limited to one wife. While that limitation sounds absurd, it was a rational attempt to avoid white intruders entering marriages of convenience with Cherokee women, which brings up another speculation about Ms. Warren's story.

The marriage application supposedly naming the Cherokee

ancestor was made in Oklahoma in 1894. Oklahoma statehood was in 1907, but 1894 would have been during the height of the white intruder problem in the Cherokee Nation, but the application was made in Logan County, Oklahoma Territory, nowhere near the Cherokee Nation.

Whatever the fact of blood, Dr. Allen has been unable to find Warren's ancestor on any Cherokee Rolls, so it would appear that the ancestor was not a citizen.

If Elizabeth Warren listed herself in the Harvard faculty directory as Indian hoping to meet others of like descent, there's no harm and no foul. Can you imagine how hard it must be to promote a stickball game on the Harvard Quad?

If she was making herself available to mentor Indian students, that would be commendable. I expect the Indian students would have said so by now.

There's no question Harvard has used Elizabeth Warren to hoist the flag of diversity. Harvard is flying a false flag and it's reprehensible.

The question, to me, is whether Elizabeth Warren was a box checker, seeking personal advantage on the backs of people who lived their lives with the down side of being Indian? The answer is probably in her personal file with the correspondence that accompanied her hiring. There's no literal box to check until after one is hired or not.

If she's guilty, it's some evidence of a character flaw and a tragedy for the 99%. But even if she turns out to be a box checker, Elizabeth Warren will never reach the category dominated in modern times by Ward Churchill.

Ward Churchill's second jury has spoken. That would be the jury in his wrongful termination lawsuit that found, not irrationally, that Churchill would still be a tenured full professor at the University of Colorado if he had not written an essay faulting the victims of the World Trade Center bombing for the location of their employment.

"Little Eichmanns," he called them, in some half-witted parody of Hannah Arendt's observations in her masterful work *Eichmann in Jerusalem: A Report on the Banality of Evil* (1963). Arendt, unlike Churchill, was an intellectual of substance and great accomplishment, and I doubt that he's read much of her writings. Had he understood *The Origins of Totalitarianism* (1951), much of what he published in his career would have been done differently. In keeping with my normal practice of revealing my biases, I admit to being most offended by Churchill's *Pacifism as Pathology: Reflections on the Role of Armed Struggle in North America* (1998). It is, perhaps, his justification for that famous photograph of the learned professor with an assault rifle. My complaint comes from having worked with Cesar Chavez, admired Martin Luther King, Jr., and spent no small amount of my life urging young Indians to train as "briefcase warriors." American Indians are oppressed peoples, now as well as historically, but the way out for us is community organizing rather than gunplay.

This fundamental disagreement about the role of an American Indian university professor colors my views of Churchill. Eichmann, Arendt famously observed, was a not particularly bright cog in a genocidal machine. Assuming everyone agrees that capitalism is a genocidal machine (although I, for one, do not), the idea that one who happens to be present in the World Trade Center is a cog in that machine is preposterous.

A college student doing an internship at a stock brokerage? A college student waiting tables at Windows on the World restaurant? Forgive my fixation on college students, but Churchill is supposed to care about them. Toting an assault rifle requires no college degree, but he is—or was—a professor.

The "little Eichmanns" absurdity brings me back to Churchill's first jury, American Indians. Maybe I don't get out enough, but I know very few Indians who were not offended enough by that remark to ask, "Who is this Indian professor?" All of the reporting styled Churchill an Indian.

While I too was offended, I remember seeing a card from the United Keetoowah Band on a website, and so I did not have anything to say about Churchill's bona fides. If the Keetoowahs wanted to claim him, I support their right to do so. It turns out they didn't. It turns out he abused their trust, and this public insult to the victims of 9-11 was more than they could stand. When they told their story, Churchill's last shred of cover as an Indian was gone.

Churchill's first jury was the Indian community, to the extent that it is a community, and that jury was not unanimous. There are individuals who are willing to claim Churchill as Indian. Last I looked, however, no individual could confer a tribal identity.

In anticipation of Churchill's apologists, let us incinerate a straw man: blood quantum.

Make a Venn diagram. One circle is Indians by blood without regard to how much blood. The other is Indians by citizenship. They overlap, but not completely. The Cherokee freedmen, those without Cherokee blood anyway, are Indians by citizenship, a Cherokee citizenship they had under Cherokee law before the 14th Amendment gave them US citizenship and, indeed, before Cherokees maintaining tribal relations had US citizenship.

The issue is not whether those two circles completely overlap. They do not. The issue is who gets to locate the circles. Churchill's idea of self-identification means individuals get to draw the circles. I say tribes get to draw the circles, and this is why I was willing to recognize Churchill as a citizen of the United Keetoowah Band if they were.

What about people who are not enrolled but claim they are "part Indian?" Count me among the wags who like to ask "Which part?" Whatever your attitude, there is nothing wrong with claiming tribal descent rather than tribal citizenship if the claim is true. It's seems to me that a claim of descent, when true, carries only the legal effect a tribe says it does and protection under the Civil Rights Act of 1964. That is, if somebody discriminates against an individual because they are thought to be Indian it does not matter whether they actually are. The Civil Rights Act protects everyone from invidious discrimination, even when it's mistaken.

So the real world is divided into Indians (tribal citizens), descendants (without regard to blood quantum), and imaginary Indians, the Ward Churchills and Andrea Smiths and Raymond Pierottis.

The imaginary Indians become particularly threatening when, like Churchill, they become highly visible in a manner that discredits everything they touch. As we speak, the Cherokee Nation is erecting a veteran's center to serve and honor returning veterans. Is this the act of a nation that considers September 11 a deserved case of chickens coming home to roost?

What can real Indians do to protect themselves against imaginary Indians? This is a lot more complicated than it sounds. In the meantime, Churchill is getting to be the age when most people consider what will be his third jury: his legacy.

It is a good thing that people remember you as somebody

who made the world better than you found it. Individuals who write and teach certainly understand that at some point, but it's easy to forget in the hurly-burly of hundreds of students at a time and "publish or perish."

Churchill is eligible for Social Security right now. He is close enough to the end of his career to sum it up or at least consider summing it up. It's at this stage when Indian people begin to be regarded as "elders," in the sense of having lived a good life of contribution to the tribal community. Or not.

Ward Churchill's case brings it up in our collective face, but most Indians in academia have had the problem of persons who "self-identify" as Indian without anything to back up the identity beyond alleged family oral history.

I have always wondered what difference it makes if the proverbial Cherokee grandmother exists? The question is worth repeating: In what sense is somebody Indian who has to hire a genealogist to find an ancestor? I'm not saying that an adult onset Indian cannot belatedly form tribal ties, but connection to a tribe for such people is the exception rather than the rule.

My own position is that Indian identity is not about what you claim but rather about who claims you. This is diametrically opposed to Churchill's idea that self-identification is what counts.
I will leave the question with a gentle suggestion for non-Indians who wish to employ Indians. Few Indians are offended by being asked if they are enrolled. If they are in fact enrolled, that should shift the burden to anybody who claims they are not Indian. If they are not enrolled, the burden should be on them to prove they are Indian by reference to some existing Indian community.

Is this rocket science?

But what is to be done about the fakes, particularly fakes who have tenure in academia? I have participated in many conversations about this, particularly with Cherokees, who seem to be the most common victims. It's odd to say this, but in my experience Cherokees are most likely to get their identity purloined but Lakotas are most likely to get their culture stolen—often by the same people.

There should be a clan for these fakers in each tribe: the Ferengi Clan. Ferengi live by the Rules of Acquisition, the number of which is subject to controversy in the Star Trek universe, but the following are relevant to the present discussion:

10. Greed is eternal.
52. Never ask when you can take.
60. Keep your lies consistent.
97. Enough...is never enough.
99. Trust is the biggest liability of all.
181. Not even dishonesty can tarnish the shine of profit.
284. Deep down everyone's a Ferengi.

You get the idea, and I hope that deep down everyone is not a Ferengi, but I have had some passing strange conversations with faux Indians that leave me at a loss to understand what they do in terms other than profit.

Affirmative action is on its last legs, but there is still an advantage to claiming Indian identity if you want to teach in an Indian studies program. Your tribal ties make research partnerships with tribal colleges easier and you might personally be able to attract and mentor Indian students, the least successful group in higher education.

It's easy to justify hiring a qualified Indian, but if that person is a fake the advantages quickly fade away. The university can only hope to discover the truth before they grant tenure.

What about Indians? Aren't we harmed by the fakes, both when they suck up the limited job opportunities and when they misrepresent us to the non-Indian world? Well, in a word, yes, but it's not an Indian problem. It's a tribal problem.

Tribes in modern times are in charge of their own rolls, and they can certainly in some cases make it easier to check out somebody who claims tribal citizenship. But until recently, I was at a loss to suggest how tribes could do anything proactive to discourage fakes.

I wish this idea were mine, but it belongs to Stacy Leeds, a Cherokee law professor who is currently the Dean of the University of Arkansas Law School. I mention it with her permission.

A tribe could bring a lawsuit in tribal court for an injunction against a fake who claims to be a tribal citizen. This kind of fraud harms the tribe's reputation.

Whoa, the lawyers will say---the tribal court has no jurisdiction. That is true only if the faker is a fake. If the faker challenges tribal jurisdiction on the grounds the faker is not part of the tribal community and not bound by tribal law, there's the self-admission of fakery. If the individual is a tribal citizen, jurisdiction can be founded both on tribal citizenship and on the fact that misrepresenting the tribe is a tort that has an impact where the tribal court is located. But if the individual is a tribal citizen, chances are we are not having this conversation.

Or, if the faker ignores the tribal court proceedings, the same result follows. The tribe gets a default judgment declaring the faker to be a fake.

Stacy Leeds' idea is nothing short of brilliant. Court orders are public records. These kinds of lawsuits can create public documents that prove to anyone's satisfaction that an individual is nothing but a member of the Ferengi Clan of the Wanabi Nation.

Hire a Ferengi at your own risk.

Everybody has ancestors. We don't pick them, but they in some sense made us who we are. It is good to honor our ancestors when they have been honorable even as we live down their faults. We don't get the choice of basking in their reflected glory while ignoring that which is inglorious or even ugly.

My full-blooded Cherokee great–grandfather Henry Teehee and my Dutch settler great-grandfather Samuel Van Hooser were on opposite sides of a social conflict about which I have strong opinions in the 21st century, but I am still descended from both of them and would never deny either.

I was thinking about this when I wrote a couple of columns about the denial of tenure at the University of Michigan to Andrea Smith, who had misrepresented herself as Cherokee.

I was thinking about this again when I saw a book forthcoming by the "Comanche scholar" Raymond Pierotti.

Prof. Pierotti had been outed by the Comanche Nation, but it's just as significant that he was outed by his own brother. This is the thing I as a mixed blood who has chosen to retain tribal citizenship have always wondered: what about the living European relatives of fake Indians? What about the European ancestors of fake Indians?

Some years ago, I was privileged to visit The Netherlands as a tourist. I had a great time and I recommend the experience, but that experience did not involve reconnection to my "Dutch roots." I have no Dutch roots. I was born and raised in Oklahoma and my known roots go back to when it was called Indian Territory. That's who I've always been and I would not go to Europe for the purpose of becoming somebody else.

For some reason, lots of folks have decided it's a good day to be indigenous. Now, I've got no problem with Prof. Pierotti writing about traditional ecological knowledge. But like every other scholar, he needs to cite his sources, and I would hope he understands that there is no pan-tribal ecological tradition. A publisher's blurb claimed that Pierotti provided "a fascinating look at the complexities of his career conducting research from an Indigenous perspective and the reluctance of many university Native programs of study to recruit natural scientists."

Native studies programs generally come in two flavors. Some have a humanities focus and some a social science focus. It's true that a natural scientist would not be an easy fit for programs asking about the representation of horses in Joy Harjo's poetry or how much jurisdiction the U.S. Supreme Court intends to leave for tribal courts.

In spite of the biases of Indian studies programs, Prof. Pierotti appears to claim that he has had "a career conducting research from an indigenous perspective." I wonder whose indigenous perspective he has been using, since the Comanche Nation repossessed theirs?

Is there a Comanche ecological tradition or a Plains Indian ecological tradition? I'm not informed at this time, but I know several real Comanches I can ask. My own research often turns on what is fair, and I don't think my ethnicity gives me seriously different ideas about what is fair.

Speaking of what is fair, I'm about to retire, and The Netherlands was a pretty nice place. And I was looking at what made Prof. Pierotti a Comanche. The argument in his family was over whether the kids were told stories about a Comanche ancestor, exactly the same argument Elizabeth Warren made about being Cherokee.

Is the issue whether the stories were in fact told? It seems tacky to call a dead person a liar, so if stories make the person, then Pierotti is Comanche and Warren is Cherokee....and I'm Dutch.

Is the issue whether the stories are in fact true? That's harder for Pierotti and Warren, but I still get to be Dutch because Samuel Van Hooser's grave is marked in a family cemetery not far from his homestead in Missouri, which I still own. Of course, I never met my Dutch ancestor just as Pierotti never met his Comanche one and Warren never met her Cherokee one, if such existed. Note that this is not about blood quantum.

Thanks to blood quantum, many Indians today take blood to be culture. A full blood is assumed to speak the language and know the history and maybe even be a non-Christian. Chop the blood degree and less cultural competence is assumed.

Blood is a metaphor, folks, and we should not confuse it with what it represents. If that's not so, then everybody with an Indian ancestor they never met is in some sense Indian. If culture doesn't count, I suppose we need not fear assimilation, because we will always have the blood.

Hot dog, I'm Dutch! I can prove it! The Netherlands has better health care than Indian Health Service and a social safety net that makes ours look like a spider web. They have a much more civilized criminal justice system, too, but I wouldn't be going there to work.

On the other hand, they have no national cuisine to speak of. No fry bread, no grape dumplings, no kanuchi or wild onions. And it's so far from my grandchildren.

Maybe the academic fakers are right. It *is* a good day to be indigenous.

10 STORIES ARE NOT THE SAME AS THINGS

I've had conversations with an Indian who is rightly concerned about a self-identified "Mohawk" with no tribal ties making a career out of selling fake indigenous artistic sensibility. I suppose the good news is that we are long past the time when the dominant culture would scoff at Indian intellectual property claims by arguing that Indians can't produce intellectual property.

The Indian Arts and Crafts Act of 1990 is a splendid law dealing with a whole other area of exploitation, the proverbial "Hopi kachina" made in Taiwan or "Zuni fetish" from Hong Kong. IACA has the most robust remedies I've seen in a federal consumer law.

And it is a consumer law. It protects tribes from having certain cultural items misrepresented but it also protects the people who want to buy Indian designed and Indian produced arts and crafts.

Anybody can visit Palo Duro Canyon, since it's a park now, and paint a portrait of Coyote howling in front of some recognizable rock. Palo Duro has significance to the history of the Kiowa and Comanche peoples who once controlled the Southern Plains and some people believe that a Kiowa or Comanche artist might have more to say though the image of Coyote in that place. Other people think that all portraits of Coyote are the same and to claim otherwise is intellectual gibberish.

My purpose is not to take sides in artistic issues but rather to say that those who think a Kiowa or Comanche person brings something special to depicting Palo Duro and are willing to pay for that unique contribution of blood memory have a right to be certain that they are not being fooled about the fact of the tribal connection.

IACA contains both criminal and civil penalties but it is a pipe dream to think US Attorney offices will ever line up to prosecute on the criminal side of the docket while dealing with the "wars" on drugs and terrorism.

However, the civil side is an untapped gold mine.

The civil penalties give standing to Indians generally, Indian tribes, and "Indian arts and crafts organizations," defined to mean marketing organizations consisting only of Indians, any tribe or several tribes.

Damages are set by IACA at three times the profit made from lying about a tribal affiliation OR $1,000 a day for every day the fake items are offered for sale. The law provides for recovery of court costs and attorney fees and for punitive damages in cases of really persistent or egregious violations. The suit can be brought by tribes or individual Indians who are being faked or by Indian arts and crafts organizations.

Ever since the law started allowing this, I have wondered why somebody does not put together a national Indian marketing co-op and fund it at first by just suing fakers? It's hard to imagine a remedy that could be put into the law that is not already there, yet we all see violations, sometimes even at tribal events. We have the tools to stop the fakers.

However, IACA is about arts and crafts, not music, stories, books, poems—intellectual property. There is no question that fakers have intruded into tribal intellectual heritages as well as crafts, but there are substantial obstacles to a law on the all-inclusive scale of IACA.

The first problem is our own. We differ over what is individual and what is collective knowledge and how to balance that with the dominant culture, where it is always individual knowledge. There is no reason a tribe cannot own copyrights and patents and trademarks, but I know of no tribe that has done so on a culture-protecting scale even though tribal enterprises register trademarks like any other business.

I presume that Tanka Bars, for example, are registered trademarks. I certainly hope so. For those unaware of this sublime

51

treat, Tanka Bars is an Indian owned and operated business selling energy bars made of bison meat and cranberries. They sell on line and they are good enough to give junk food the bad name it deserves.

On the other hand, there are too many Cherokee trademarks to count. Jeep is only a big one. Lots of Apaches as well. Few of these businesses have anything to do with real Cherokees or Apaches, but the thing about trademarks is that if you don't protect them you lose the right to protect them. It's not a fair rule against peoples who until recently had no real access to the legal system. It's like the ruling against the Oneida Nation's land claims that they failed to assert those claims at a time when they were in no position to assert anything. But it's the rule and lots of folks have spent money building up trade names with advertising that they would resist having tribes swoop in and claim on the cheap.

What about music and the written word?

The First Amendment generally protects the right to utter lies but it does not protect from having to pay damages that the lies cause. This is a good rule because anything less puts the government in the position of deciding what is true. That's not up to the government, federal or state or tribal.

Who is harmed by fake Indian prose, poetry, or music? Real Indian artists, but only in the sense that art is a zero sum game. That is, artists face limited markets and fierce competition. This is the fact of the matter, says the Indian poet who has won a major competition (Native Writers Circle of the Americas) but never found a publisher while many fakes have whizzed by me in the fast lane. But how in the world can I prove that if Princess Cherokee Sunflower Hair Spray had not published her book I would have published mine?

We know at the gut level that Indian fakers are misrepresenting in a manner that will affect tribes in the long run, because books and recordings tend to crowd out performances. In the long run, the real culture is swallowed by the fake one.

Tribes are harmed and Indian writers and composers are harmed. Even though I am an individual Indian so far on the political outs with my tribal government I can't have a book signing on the Cherokee National Holiday, I still think the power to represent cultural heritage must reside in tribes rather than individuals. The open question is how to draft a constitutional law to assert that power.

I'm not sure that can be done. If I'm correct, then consumers of books and music will be on the firmest ground that matters if they are certain that what they buy moves them. Art works at the human level or it does not, and it's hard to see how a tribal trademark would improve it.

11 SELLING MAGIC; DELIVERING DEATH

James Ray's Arizona trial for manslaughter played like a bad movie, Harry Potter meets John Wayne. For $9,695, Ray promised that Native American wisdom imparted by him, a white man, would make you healthy, wealthy, and wise. People lined up to consume this swill in spite of the obvious fact that most real Indians are neither healthy nor wealthy. Wisdom is in the eye of the beholder but we have enough sense not to kill people in spiritual ceremonies.

Dennis Mehravar, one of the suckers, er, participants, quoted Ray: "He asked, 'Has anybody been in a sweat lodge before?' I would say probably maybe eight or nine people raised their hands. And then his comment was, 'well, you've never been to *my* sweat lodge.'"

I'm Cherokee, and our purification ceremony involves water rather than heat. It's also not for sale, although there's not a lot to be done if somebody decided to sell it and did not care about lost reputation in the Cherokee communities.

I've participated in sweats conducted by Comanche, Cheyenne, and Lakota, but I've never seen plastic used in the construction of a sweat lodge, which was apparently the case in Arizona.

In Ray's plastic tent, three people died and eighteen were admitted to hospitals. I've never even seen that many people in a sweat lodge at one time.

Ray considered the ceremony a near-death experience. The first time I sweated, the elder in charge told me to leave if I had trouble.

The whole Ray debacle reminded me of another death in the early nineties here in Central Texas. A woman died in a "Native American sweat lodge" maintained by a non-Indian while sweating *by herself.* No fire keeper. No singer. Nobody to remove her if she was unable to remove herself.

In spite of the fact that no Indian was involved, the tragic death brought calls to ban dangerous, pagan ceremonies. Those of us who leaped to the defense found ourselves cross-examined on the fine points of the sweat lodge. This is Comanche country, but I doubt any Comanche ever died in a sweat. It would be hard to take the conversation seriously if real people were not dead.

There's a big legal problem around the abuse of Indian ceremonies that ties into the cultural problems we all experience.

Government has the power to ban practices that are in fact dangerous. To put a finer point on it, practices that a reasonable legislator might have believed were dangerous. Dead people are pretty strong evidence of danger.

To defend against the banning, we have to delve into matters of how the ceremonies are done that most of us consider private. Indian spiritual practices differ from Christianity in that most of us have some idea like the one taught me: "The spirit world takes care of it's own business." That is, trying to convert others is silly and futile.

The Indian equivalent of the TV preacher gets no respect. A Comanche medicine man, now deceased, who was kind enough to teach me a little about the people on whose bones I walk here in Texas, had more holes in his jeans than teenagers put there on purpose. I never saw him charge anything beyond expenses but I did see him refuse to reveal things and make merciless sport of anthropologists.

A lot of what is written about Indian ceremonies is unreliable. You can only learn by doing and those who know will not teach weekend Indians.

Why not ban the ceremonies when abused by non-Indians? Because the First Amendment protects all beliefs. A non-Indian may hold beliefs he takes to be traditionally Indian in a completely sincere manner, but the courts generally do not inquire into sincerity.

Sincerity?   Look no farther than the tragedy in Arizona.

Those people paid a lot of money. They were explicitly instructed that they would think they were going to die and they should not interfere with how others processed the experience.

According to some survivors, Ray's staff floated the idea that the dead people had left their bodies on purpose and were having such a good time they decided not to come back! *That's* sincerity.

Indians seeking a way out of being blamed for abuse of ceremonies they don't want public in the first place have one weapon. The First Amendment, like the rest of the US Constitution, does not apply to Indian nations. The First Amendment bans "establishment of religion," and for many tribes spiritual practices established from time immemorial are the glue holding them together.

Tribal governments can ban the sale of ceremonies. This ban could only be applied to tribal citizens but it could arguably be applied to them wherever they are. If they put the tribe's spiritual heritage up for sale, disenroll them, so that they may claim to be healthy, wealthy, and wise, but not to be Indian.

By that action, tribal governments can effectively cancel the Indian trademark on the ceremony. James Ray, of course, never claimed to be Indian. Those who would pay almost ten grand for esoteric Indian knowledge claimed by a non-Indian display a degree of stupidity for which there is no legal cure.

The object of kicking people out of the tribe who purport to trade in things that are not for sale is not to protect people too foolish to be reached by mere logic. The object is to protect ourselves from being tarnished by the foolishness and to keep that which we believe to be sacred, sacred.

12 BORN AND RAISED FOR DEATH ROW

Capital punishment, the saying goes, means that those without the capital get the punishment, and over 35 years of labor in criminal law has yet to show me a case that disproves it. Court-appointed lawyers usually defend capital cases, because prosecutors do not typically choose to seek the death penalty against defendants who can afford the stratospheric legal fees of a capital defense.

The only capital case I defended in private practice was one of the very few I've seen where the lawyers were hired rather than appointed, and we won—victory being defined in that instance as the government was not allowed to kill our client.

Death row, like most poor neighborhoods, has a disproportionate number of minority residents. Those of us who come from poor neighborhoods know that there are mean people there, and plenty of conditions that make even good people mean. We also know that the vast majority of poor people survive those conditions without becoming mean.

It's this hearty survival rate of poor people justifies in the minds of some what they call "putting down the mad dogs," in spite of the fact that it is much more expensive to kill sociopaths than it is to lock them up without the possibility of parole. Those are the two choices for dealing with the people who have become too dangerous to live among us, and such people do exist—in all my years of practice, I have had contact with three of them; three out of the thousands of criminal defendants with whom I have dealt.

Based on my many years in the legal system, I do not trust it to pick those three sociopaths out of a crowd. Sociopaths, you see, are not always poor people—some of them are even white. Back in the days (within my lifetime) when we had the death penalty for rape, those executed were most often dark-skinned men accused of raping white women, and thanks to DNA exonerations we now understand that cross-racial identification is highly unreliable. Even utterly certain eyewitnesses make mistakes, and confessions are so notoriously unreliable that everyone understands why police investigators withhold some details of every crime that makes the newspaper. The more publicity the crime gets, the more disturbed people will line up to confess. Making things even more confusing is that confessions by persons actually involved in a crime are often given to shift blame, leading to the perverse outcome in some capital cases that the more experienced criminal is able to make a deal to escape the death penalty by testifying against a less savvy co-defendant, without regard to which defendant was more culpable.

Since eyewitness identifications and confessions can be unreliable, it's easy to see why there are very few trials where everybody agrees on what happened. What may appear crystal clear in the newspapers can only be seen in the courtroom as through a glass, darkly.

A lawyer's first duty in a capital case is to tell the best story that can be told with the facts as they stand. If you are a juror in such a case, you have buckets of messy facts brought into the courtroom and must listen to lawyers who assemble stories from those facts—often without regard to what they may believe to be the truth.

A lawyer's second duty in a capital case, should the first not be discharged successfully, is to make absolutely sure that the jury fully understands the life they are being asked to end. Jurors are introduced to a man by way of the worst thing he's done in his life, a circumstance that would be a mighty challenge to any of us, even if the task were less vital than to befriend twelve strangers who have nothing in common but their sworn willingness to kill you if the government gives them a good enough reason.

All this brings me to an Indian I want you to know better than his jury did—Douglas Ray Stankewitz, the longest tenured inmate on California's death row. Like most Indians who find themselves in a group of non-Indians, he is currently known as "Chief," but unlike many Indians, he is proud of the nickname.

The government wants to kill Chief because Theresa Greybeal was shot dead in the course of a robbery by a group of people high on heroin, and there is no question that Chief was one of them.

There is a serious question about who pulled the trigger, and juries are reluctant to kill individuals who did not pull the trigger. But as far as his jury knew, Douglas Stankewitz pulled the trigger, and he might have, but we will never know, based on his trial.

Just as you can't discuss federal Indian policy without recourse to history, it's hard to understand Douglas Stankewitz and his crimes outside of his historical context, which includes the spectacular destruction of California Indians by white settlers, a destruction that persisted well into the 20th century and with which the survivors still struggle.

Douglas Ray "Chief" Stankewitz is a citizen of the Big Sandy Rancheria, as they call reservations in California. He was born on May 31, 1958, to Marion Sample Stankewitz, the sixth of her eleven children. She was the fifth of seven children. Her father, Sam Jack Sample, was Mono and Chukchansi, and her mother was Mono. She met Douglas's father, a truck driver of Polish descent, when she was picking grapes and he was her supervisor. They were both practicing drunks.

Douglas was born the year the Big Sandy Rancheria was "terminated" as part of the national policy to force Indians to assimilate. In other words, for most of the time that the young Douglas was being let down by the adults around him, the Big Sandy Rancheria did not exist in the eyes of the federal government. His mother had also been raised on the Big Sandy Rancheria, a place until recently blighted by poverty, alcohol abuse and hopelessness. Marion drank beer by the case while pregnant, and when Douglas was born his father was in jail for beating his mother. His mother had no prenatal care—she first saw a doctor regarding her pregnancy when she was in labor.

Douglas was beaten regularly by both of his parents and was taken to the emergency room three times before his first birthday. At age six, he was found injured and wandering on the streets. The police took him home, where his mother admitted to having beaten him. The police did not remove him from the home, apparently because they decided that the process would have been too complicated. There were nine children in the home at the time, and Douglas's father was in jail.

Less than three months later, Douglas was brought to the police station by a neighbor who found the boy on his doorstep, again injured. This time, all the children were taken away and Marion was jailed.

After two unsuccessful foster home placements—the foster parents were unable to deal with Douglas's violent emotional eruptions—the seven-year-old was committed to Napa State Psychiatric Hospital for 90 days. While he received no treatment there (beyond being diagnosed with a severe emotional disturbance), this placement was extended twice, for a total of nine months. This child trapped in an adult institution became easy prey for sexual assault, and that became an unfortunate part of his "education."

He was then placed in a foster home, where he stayed for nearly four years, the second longest stay at one address he has had in his life. The longest was in is his current address: San Quentin's death row. He received no visits from his natural family during that placement with the foster family. His foster mother had to make a personal plea to get Douglas into the third grade:

The day I went to pick him up, I'll never forget. He went down on all fours in a corner, growling and snorting at me. On the way home, he jumped over into the back seat and clawed all the stuffing out of the upholstery. When we walked into the kitchen of my home, he shuffled over to the dish rack, full of dry dishes, and threw the whole thing across the room. I had been told not to physically restrain or punish him because he would go berserk if touched, but I figured he was already berserk, so being as big as I am, I just grabbed him from behind, wrapped my whole self around him, down we went and I just held on for dear life until he calmed down. It's taken me all this time to tame him. I've taught him to talk instead of grunt, to use the toilet, to dress himself, to use silverware, to take care of animals without hurting them, to ask instead of grab... He's been begging me to teach him to read and write and do numbers like the other foster kids, so I think he's ready for school... Will you take him in your class? If he's any trouble, just call and I'll come pick him up.

It is unclear how this foster placement ended, and Chief is in no position to know because of his age at the time. Apparently, the state was motivated by a bureaucratic imperative to keep families together when possible, regardless of the circumstances. What is clear is that from 1970 until his first commitment to the California Youth Authority in 1972, Douglas had at least 13 placements. The longest was for five months. The first was back with his mother, where he learned to sniff paint.

For a short period, he was placed with an aunt back on the reservation, where he lived until her children were taken away because of her drunkenness. The aunt said that before Douglas came to live with her, "a lot of times there was no food in the house. Sometimes we'd save our oatmeal for [the children] because they had nothing." While Douglas was living with his aunt, his mother was sent to prison for manslaughter.

At age 13, Douglas got his first criminal referral to juvenile court. His earlier visits to juvenile court had been as what the state called a "child in need of supervision." Douglas had apparently been running with some adults, and when they showed up too late to get fed at a Fresno soup kitchen one day, the adults decided to rob someone to get money for food. Douglas involved himself in this crime by going though the victim's pockets.

Between 1972 and 1977, Douglas spent all but eight months in either Youth Authority lockups or the Sacramento County Jail. In a little over two months from the time he was released until the arrest that landed him on death row, Douglas Stankewitz consumed (according to the individuals around him) massive quantities of marijuana, alcohol, methamphetamine and heroin. At the time of the killing that brought him to death row, he had not slept for at least two days.

Chief has now spent 35 years of his life on California's death row, but virtually all of his life before arriving there was spent under the "supervision" of the state of California in one guise or another. We don't know what the jury on his trial would have made of this, but we do know that Chief's American Indian identity made their decision to kill him inevitable. That statement may seem shocking, but so are the actions of Douglas Stankewitz's court-appointed lawyer, the ex-judge Hugh Goodwin.

Since I am a retired judge and know something of the work, I was prepared to think an ex-judge from a criminal court might make a good defense attorney in a capital case, if he had the stomach for it. The problem is that Goodwin became an *ex*-judge because of his predilection for sentencing criminal defendants to go to church. He was convinced that his job as a judge was to bring people to Jesus. It is clear from reviewing the Stankewitz case that he saw his duty as a criminal defense lawyer the same way.

The fearsome responsibility of a capital defense can keep a lawyer awake at night, but Mr. Goodwin's sleep was apparently less troubled than mine, because he took the attitude that his client's life was in God's hands rather than his own.

Because there was no question that his client was involved in the killing—only whether he pulled the trigger—Mr. Goodwin had ample notice that the main business of this trial would be in the penalty phase. There was much that the jury should have been told in the penalty phase, but Mr. Goodwin did not deem it important to inform them that his client had been born with fetal alcoholism syndrome, beaten, starved, sexually assaulted and deprived of any loving relationship with an adult.

Instead, he called to the stand a jailer and an assistant district attorney to give their opinions that anybody can reform if they allow the Christian God to come into their life. Predictably, the cross-examination of these witnesses bored in on whether they had any reason to believe Douglas Stankewitz had invited God into his life. They did not.

Errors by a lawyer do not require reversal if the lawyer had a tactical reason for making the errors. Hugh Goodwin swore to this statement about his tactics in that trial:

I have never believed in the separation of church and state, as I made clear when I was a judge. I recognize that this is a controversial view which is not widely shared. When I presented the testimony of a Deputy District Attorney and the Fresno County Jail chaplain that they believed people could be transformed by the power of God if they let God into their lives, I knew that it was likely that on cross-examination they would state that there was no evidence that Mr. Stankewitz would let God into his life. Nonetheless, I believed that by presenting this testimony, God's will would be done, and accordingly I did so.

As idiotic as the "power of God" defense was in a capital murder case, it would have had a prayer of swaying a jury against death if there were a shred of evidence that Douglas Stankewitz had a Christian bone in his body. But Douglas "Chief" Stankewitz is a Mono Indian, born on the Big Sandy Rancheria, raised by the State of California in a parade of incompetent foster homes, mental hospitals and juvenile facilities. His grandfather, Sam Jack Sample, was a ceremonial singer and medicine man who died singing in the roundhouse when Douglas was a small boy. Goodwin might as well have entrusted his client's life to Zoroaster or appealed to the beliefs of Jainism for all the chance his client had of grabbing hold of that lifeline.

The defense in a capital case must compel the jury to understand the life they are being asked to end. In this case, the jury was told that goodness is linked to being Christian, and the defense lawyer might as well have said plainly that the only good Indians he ever saw were dead.

At this writing, the Big Sandy Rancheria has regained federal recognition and has opened a casino. Using those casino funds, they finally have an office to enforce the Indian Child Welfare Act. They also have a Head Start program.

In another case of poor timing, the name of Sam Jack Sample, Douglas's grandfather, has turned up on the list of persons for whom the Department of the Interior is holding property in trust. Since Stankewitz's mother is deceased, he may actually inherit that property, thereby acquiring the funds to pay for his funeral—if he had anyone to attend it.

Chief Stankewitz has no execution date set and the litigation to get him a new trial continues. Until he does get a fair trial, we won't have any basis to say whether he is among the worst of the worst who deserve the death penalty or whether he is just another man without the capital getting the punishment.

On October 29, 2012, the US Court of Appeals for the Ninth Circuit held, in a 2-1 opinion, that Douglas Stankewitz is entitled to a new trial of the punishment phase because his lawyer failed to investigate or to present to the jury substantial mitigating evidence. California can ask for a rehearing en banc, then an appeal to the US Supreme Court. If California loses, it can either re-try the punishment phase or agree that Chief should be sentenced to life in prison.

13 IN MEMORY OF JAY SPOTTED ELK

In my time as a trial judge, I've learned that often when a litigant says it's not about the money it's in fact about the money. You can't tell at the beginning of a case, but you can tell at the end. In this case, it was not about the money.

An Indian hanging himself in the drunk tank is seldom big news in Indian Country except to his relatives. When Jay Spotted Elk hung himself while facing misdemeanor charges in Sheridan County, Nebraska, his mother decided not to stand for it. Arlyn Eastman/Broken Nose sued the county and several individuals who might have been able to prevent the suicide if they had been properly trained and motivated.

Any lawsuit is difficult, and this one much more so. In the wake of the civil rights movement, there was a time when the courts seemed generally sympathetic to claims by the powerless against the powerful. As a result, the Republican Party took on the reorientation of the federal courts as a project that continues to this day. The result has been the racial attacks on Sonia Sotomayor and the hearing on the appointment of Elena Kagan that left the Republicans on the Judiciary Committee praising Kagan's qualifications and personality while still resolved to vote against her (excepting Sen. Lindsey Graham (R-SC), who seemed to have found good government more important than party discipline).

In all GOP administrations since Richard Nixon, most nominees have been very young and very conservative. Young because federal judgeships are lifetime appointments and conservative to get the law back into what they choose to call the mainstream, where you can tell the winners largely by race and by class.

At this time, as at the beginning of the Bill Clinton Administration, there are no American Indians serving on federal courts, which is where Indian interests are normally adjudicated. As bad, the influx of judges with a political agenda has had approximately forty years to work its magic, since the Democrats in power during that time have been centrists who would correctly claim that stacking courts is bad government and refrain from fighting fire with fire.

I was educated in the legal landscape peopled by Thurgood Marshall (demonized in the first day of the Kagan hearings), William O. Douglas, William Brennan, and judges like Hugo Black, who wrote the words that Indian lawyers call the all-purpose Indian law dissent: "Great Nations, like great men, should keep their word." I doubt that I would have become a lawyer had Thurgood Marshall not existed and I was reluctant to wash my hand again after William O. Douglas shook it.

In modern times, the "liberals" are conservative appointees who were enlightened by their experiences on the court like Harry Blackmun or David Souter. The "center" has been moved by political calculation. As a result, people without power have a set of problems that go far beyond the fact that they often don't know lawyers and that lawsuits cost a lot of money.

Should she find a lawyer to work on a "contingent fee" (no pay unless you win), Spotted Elk's mother would have to contend with the social fact of suing a local government (the law enforcement part, no less) and with the legal fact that if there is one class of litigants that have less success than American Indians it would have to be prisoners.

The courts, since the heyday of civil rights lawsuits, have made it harder to sue local governments for damages. It's not enough that law enforcement officers violate your rights and they work for the city or the county you want to sue. To hold the local government responsible, you must prove that they did or failed to do something in particular. Most common is a failure to properly train or supervise the officers, but this has to be a pattern. One bad outcome is not enough, even if somebody is killed.

The lawyer who took on this case, Maren Chaloupka, hit a

mother lode of evidence that was good for the lawsuit but bad for the Indian community in Nebraska:

*Twelve inmates had attempted suicide in the same jail, all but one Indian.

*The inmates had attempted suicide repeatedly.

*One inmate literally killed himself the day after he told corrections officers that he no longer wanted to live.

When nothing was done in the face of all this, it was bad for the Indians who might be in the jail from time to time but it made proving that the county had failed to take suicide precautions the proverbial slam dunk. It became possible to prove that Jay Spotted Elk's last night on earth was not unusual in the history of Sheridan County, Nebraska.

According to a report in the *Scottsbluff Star-Herald*, Spotted Elk threatened suicide before he even got to the jail. Yet his belt was not removed and he was not closely watched.

In these rare cases when there's a good chance of prevailing in a trial, there comes a time when you know why the lawsuit was filed. Everybody knows that going to trial is a crapshoot, but there is something to negotiate about if the lawyer on the other side is sane. If the case settles, that's when you learn why the case was brought.

Maren Chaloupka of Scottsbluff and her co-counsel, Robin Zephier of the Abourezk Law Firm in Rapid City, got $100,000 paid to Jay Spotted Elk's estate, managed by his mother. If that was all, it would be better than not placing any cost on Indian lives, but I would be unlikely to be writing about it. The rest of the settlement requires the county to:

*Have all employees of the sheriff and jail trained in suicide prevention.

*Make efforts to contact the tribal suicide prevention program for any Indian who expresses ideas of suicide.

*Post the contact information for suicide prevention at Pine Ridge and Rosebud at the booking desk and keep a log of calls made to those programs.

*Notify the closest tribal suicide prevention program in cases where no program can be reached for the inmate's tribe.

*Allow a representative of the tribal suicide prevention program to speak to the inmate by telephone or in person and document the reason why any recommendation by the tribal suicide prevention program is not followed.

*Provide a written report on compliance with the agreement every year until 2015, after which the Spotted Elk's mother retains the right to inspect the records.

This is what civil rights lawyers can do now and then even when the courts are so stacked against them and local officials would plainly not care to spend money protecting Indians if they had a choice. In this case, we won't know exactly whose life was saved but it is safe to say that saving lives will be the result. It's for that result we should remember the life of Jay Spotted Elk.

14 HOARDING SOCIAL CAPITAL

Political scientist Robert Putnam is famous for the concept "social capital." He did not coin the term but popularized it in his book *Bowling Alone*, chronicling the diminution of social capital in modern America. Where it exists, social capital keeps us from having to lock our doors and from needing institutions to care for orphans and the elderly. A society that is rich in social capital, as we used to be, can endure shortages of economic capital. My grandmother used to tell me about the Great Depression that few people had anything, but those who did, shared.

Some reservations exist in a permanent depression. There are few jobs and tribal government controls those that exist.

In a society with high social capital, the crime rate would stay low, incomes likewise, and the sick and elderly would lack nothing that could be provided by labor. The able-bodied unemployed would keep the wood chopped and the water hauled and the roof patched with whatever materials could be put together. (Mashed tin cans will work for shingles in a pinch.)

In a society with low social capital, competition for the few jobs is fought by political means and whether you work depends on whom you know rather than your skills. Alcohol and drugs pass the time, young people go unsupervised, and the crime rate does exactly what you would expect. You have a rural version of the inner city.

If your tribal nation is rich in social capital, good for you.

If not, you have to decide what to do if you don't want to

leave. The United States has plenty of ideas for you.

First, you can ban alcohol and drugs from your community if you believe you are so different from the U.S. that the result will not be the creation of a new criminal class with money to entice your children outside the law.

Second, you can forget your traditions of restorative justice and adopt the white folks' idea of retributive justice. After all, retribution has worked so well for the U.S. that it imprisons more people per capita than any other country.

Those tribes that had no restorative justice traditions had only punishment of the body: torture or death. No Indian nation locked people up for longer than it took to sober up a drunk.

In modern times, banishment is the equivalent of the death penalty and it has the advantage of being reversible if you make a mistake, as you certainly will because every justice system does. Banishment from an Indian community with little social capital is probably a sentence to a big city neighborhood of the same character. Failure to banish is a judgment call that someone who has offended against the community is ready to contribute social capital rather than expend it. The character of the community is the sum of all individual decisions about who helps and who hurts.

Social capital can be regained. Many tribes have awakened to the links between language retention and their peoplehood and so they spend money to encourage elders to "talk Indian" to youngsters. History preservation tends to preserve social capital, too, since most of us have some ordeal in our past that binds us together as long as we have the memory.

Assimilation forces, like so many cultural tsunamis, have hit most east coast tribes. Most Oklahoma tribes are victims of both removals from lands once considered sacred and then involuntary allotment of reservation lands. When and if they acquire the means, these culturally battered peoples do not hesitate to spend on preserving what is left and regaining what can be regained.

The Mashantucket Pequots, stereotypical "rich" casino Indians, have spent lavishly on restoration of their roots. Why do they need restoring? Well, if you read *Moby Dick*, you might remember the ship was called the "Pequod." That is a variant on Pequot and a tipoff to readers of Herman Melville's time that the ship was doomed, like the Pequots. Or not, if the modern Pequots have their way.

While social capital and economic capital are not the same thing, a strong economy helps. The Cherokee Nation has problems, but we are the strongest employer in Northeastern Oklahoma and our minimum wage is higher than Oklahoma's. We do spend money on language and history, and we do honor Cherokee speakers and craftsmen. I am told that the Eastern Band does the same with resources from Mr. Harrah's casino.

Then there are lucky tribes like the Navajo Nation. With a large population (which my tribe has) and a clan system very much alive (which my tribe does not have) and a reservation that includes their sacred geography (which my tribe, among many, does not have), they are strong in language and customs. As a lawyer, I envy their court system, which has managed to command respect among knowledgeable mainstream legal scholars without forfeiting their customs.

Just as one size has never fit all in federal Indian policy, there are culture-specific limitations on how much tribal policy will transplant to other Indian nations. However, it seems to me just as likely that tribal policies will transplant as that federal or state policies will. Those tribal governments that have crime and other social cohesion problems, it seems to me, would do as well to look to their peers for models as to transplant ideas from the colonists.

I could be wrong about all this. Whether the colonists have cures for the ills they brought is open to question by reasonable people. Putnam is of course a white man and "social capital" is an imaginary concept that may have nothing to do with Indian Country. Just because prohibition and prison did not improve white society does not mean they can't improve Indian society, and they are, after all, as traditional as fry bread and at least as good for you.

15 FOX NEWS CAUSES HELL TO FREEZE OVER

Hell has officially frozen over when I rise to defend the Bureau of Indian Affairs. I was born and raised in Oklahoma, among peoples whose opinion of the BIA ranged from gang of thieves to gang that can't shoot straight to some descriptions unsuitable for a family publication. So why would I defend the BIA?

The occasion is a question raised by the right libertarian fringe in the person of John Stossel. "Why," Stossel asked, "is there a Bureau of Indian Affairs? There is no Bureau of Puerto Rican Affairs or Black Affairs or Irish Affairs. And no group in America has been more helped by the government than the American Indians, because we have the treaties, we stole their land. But 200 years later, no group does worse."

He got that last thing right, but let's think about the "help" we have gotten.

There was exile of all Indians to the west side of the Mississippi for our own protection, wild people sent off to live in a wild land, never mind that many of the tribes force marched to Indian Territory had more education and better incomes than the colonists who took over their property.

There were also reservations, where we could live on government rations and under armed guard, except for the children, who were taken away for their own good and taught the science of racial inferiority.

Those who resisted being helped? They wanted us dead.

Then those terrible pictures of the massacre at Wounded Knee ended that policy.

If containment and killing were off the table, the next possibility was forced assimilation. Tribal recognition would be "terminated" and the residents of reservations would be "relocated." To say that termination and relocation worked out well for Indians would be like saying Stossel's employer, Fox News, is fair and balanced.

In 1928, *The Problem of Indian Administration*, known in history as the Merriam Report, documented the dire condition of Indian America. Another government report twenty years later sent me to the dictionary to understand the word "inanition" as a cause of death.

What do these disasters for Indians have in common? Except for physical extermination, they were all undertaken for high-minded motives, to help the poor savages.

If there were no Bureau of Indian Affairs in the Department of the Interior, Indians would indeed be in the eyes of the US government just another special pleading ethnic group, a collection of individuals with individual rights.

As Vine Deloria, Jr. wrote back in 1969, while the black civil rights movement swirled around us, blacks have a legitimate demand for integration but Indians have a legitimate demand for separation. We are tribal peoples. If we wish to become individuals rather than part of our people, we always have the choice of severing tribal relations and taking ourselves out of the category the Constitution called "Indians not taxed."

Most of us are now taxed. Leaving the reservation no longer requires the permission of the Indian agent, and when we leave the same civil rights laws that blacks fought and died for protect us. African-Americans have our gratitude for that but their success does not protect us from the John Stossels of the world.

Can Indians be capitalists? Sure. Look at the Mississippi Choctaws, the Ho-Chunks, and the Oneida Nation that publishes *Indian Country Today*, where this essay first appeared.

Can Indians screw up? Big time. Look at casino wealth. In some nations, every child is born with guaranteed access to as much education as she can absorb and every tribal citizen who wants a job has one. In others, the seed corn goes to per capita payments, the kids get a new truck at age eighteen, and relatives are disenrolled to make bigger payments for a few greedheads.

You know what, Stossel? We're entitled to make our own errors. We've suffered enough from yours.

If there were no BIA, there would be no way for our governments to deal with the US government, unless Congress would like to take on the work. Our nations span this continent with different languages, different cultures, different degrees of economic development, and—most importantly—different aspirations.

The prosperity of this country is built on land stolen from Indians at a time when land directly represented wealth. The treaties we keep waving in your face were the legal fig leaves covering that theft. With some exceptions, we are not demanding the land back but just to be left alone on what land we have left.

Does the government owe Indians a living forever? No, not as individuals. Like the descendants of slaves, there comes a time when we have to compete with you as individuals. Our tribal nations are a different matter entirely.

What is fair, Mr. Stossel, to a people forced to live upon lands inadequate to support them? At the time of these transactions, the whole idea was to force dependence on the US government, but now you complain that we are dependent.

You express the opinion that we should be allowed to mortgage reservation land to develop it. If we can't pay, what then? Before you run your mouth about pledging our land for cash, see if you can make a computer give you a graphic of Indian land within the US over time. Watch the incredible shrinking land base.

The question is not why the Bureau of Indian Affairs? More to the point would be why not a Bureau of Crackpot White People Trying to Help Indians Affairs? We might be better off, but then hell would truly have frozen over.

16 LIVE TRUTH TO SEEK JUSTICE

The traditions of my people teach that acting unjustly toward others will cause blowback. This is famously illustrated in the story of how disease came to Man in retaliation for what he had done to parts of creation he could dominate. Man had mistaken the power to do something for the morality of doing it. Our stories warn against this hubris, and I expect yours do as well.

We like to think that this balance, what the Asian Indians call *karma*, plays out in this life. It failed the day when the North Korean government chose a day to announce the death of "Dear Leader" Kim Jong Il—a man who will be remembered for starving children in the service of acquiring nuclear weapons---that bigfooted the death of a man who actually deserved the "dear leader" appellation, Václav Havel. Kim Jong Il went to his reward on a Saturday, but his sclerotic government could not put their story together to announce it until Monday, the day after Havel made the journey.

Havel was the playwright who became a head of state with the demise of his Communist opponents in the Velvet Revolution, and some will argue that his greatest failure as head of state was presiding over the division of Czechoslovakia into The Czech Republic and Slovakia, a division that objectively makes no economic sense.

In fact, when faced with shedding the blood of the people he was elected to lead or at least adopting some of the tactics he had opposed all his life, Havel achieved a victory for the politics of truth by letting the Slovaks go in peace.

Indians should honor Havel not for his plays but for his 1978 essay, *The Power of the Powerless*, which could have been written for us because it was written for all who find their historical peoplehood in jeopardy.

Havel wrote from a time that would be, for us, before the Indian New Deal and earlier, but we can recognize life in a dictatorship in our historical experience: government appointed by the bosses, jobs apportioned to those considered "reliable," documents needed to leave the reservation, Indian testimony discounted in the colonial courts. We are not there anymore, but the feel of it is in our blood, the time when meaningful political activity was at the risk of your livelihood or your life.

"If we are to change our world view," wrote Havel, "images have to change. The artist now has a very important job to do. He's not a little peripheral figure entertaining rich people, he's really needed."

Do our artists speak to that need? I give you Elizabeth Cook-Lynn, N. Scott Momaday, Carter Revard, Jim Northrup, Joy Harjo, Tomson Highway, Johnny Rustywire—the list could go on for pages. Even Sherman Alexie, who does entertain rich people, has also supported the liberation of Indians from all stereotype, all the time, and much of Alexie's entertainment value is rooted in demonstrating the absurdity of our current relations with the colonists.

Havel's seminal essay about freedom cannot be meaningfully condensed in the space I have, but if I have one sentence I choose "Truth as a weapon." The motto Havel put forward was "Truth and love must prevail over lies and hate."

Note that he said "must prevail" rather than "will prevail." The man was not crazy. He lived though 1968, when Russian tanks rolled into Czechoslovakia and ended the "Prague Spring."

Havel again: "Work for something because it is good, not just because it stands a chance to succeed. "

What his essay has to say to Indian people is that if you are still a people, act like it. Disobey the attempt to control your life until the attempt to control your life begins to exact a price the United States is unwilling to pay. If your peoplehood is a truth, live that truth.

"The exercise of power is determined by thousands of

interactions between the world of the powerful and that of the powerless, all the more so because these worlds are never divided by a sharp line: everyone has a small part of himself in both."

Havel's life teaches that first the artists break the mold the powerless are supposed to inhabit. Our artists have done that.

Then other intellectuals begin to demonstrate that, in so many words, the emperor is buck-naked. Vine Deloria, Jr. opened this process for us. Many have followed his example, and you have read people with dominant culture credentials demonstrating the fraudulent nature of what Seneca law professor Robert Odawi Porter calls "federal Indian control law." Steven Newcomb and Peter d'Errico have done yeoman work in reducing complex lies to 800 words of truth in *Indian Country Today*. Matthew L. M. Fletcher is an intellectual dynamo roaring out of the Grand Traverse Band of Ottawa and Chippewa Indians into books, law reviews, and his *Turtle Talk* blog.

We have the artistic and intellectual firepower to raise the banner of truth.

The politicians, of course, are always last to join the party, but join they will or become irrelevant. This is the lesson I draw from the life of Václav Havel, beside whom Kim Jong Il is bovine excrement on the boot heels of history.

17 EDUCATION BY GIRLS

In 2012, I was watching and thinking about Gabrielle Douglas, the teenaged heroine of the London Olympics. Or so I view her. I was thinking of Olga Korbut, Nadia Comaneci, Mary Lou Retton, Shannon Miller---all young girls who taught us that tough is not just a masculine trait.

I was looking forward to seeing Gabby Douglas on the Wheaties box. I have granddaughters.

Then there was the uproar about her hair. Really, America?

Then there was the uproar about her mother's bankruptcy. Hey, America, if Gabby's mom had the sum the Romneys spent training and feeding Rafalca the dressage horse, she would not have gone bankrupt. I hate to break it to you, but since 2008 a lot of hard working people have gone bankrupt in lesser endeavors than boosting a daughter towards Olympic gold.

I mean no disrespect towards Rafalca. As the Cherokee cowboy Will Rogers said, "A man that don't love a horse, there's something the matter with him." It may be a rich man's sport, but Rafalca is a fine animal and if she were mine, wild horses could not keep me from watching her dance.

Then there was an uproar that Gabby Douglas wore a pink leotard rather than red, white, or blue. Like Michelle Obama before her, she's "unpatriotic," goes the narrative.

What is this urge white Americans always have for black Americans, not to mention American Indians, to prove their "patriotism?" America, your involuntary citizens from Africa or

Native America prove their patriotism every day they don't set out to kill you.

If that's shocking, and you just can't wrap your mind around the history of white people vis-a-vis African-Americans and Indians, then can you wrap your mind around the history of disturbed individuals and mass murder?

Make yourself two lists.

Including political motivations or not is arguable, since people who commit mass murder for political reasons are in my view no less disturbed, but I understand reasonable people can differ.

Put aside those who kill without racial selection of victims.

But then you are left with how many times a black or an Indian since, say, Nat Turner, has set out on a mission of wholesale slaughter of white people.

Now think about how many disturbed white people have engaged in wholesale slaughter of black people or Indians, and to be fair in light of the last paragraph we can exclude Chivington and Custer. Wounded Knee I, a massacre of noncombatant Indians in 1890, might be a fair cut off date, since that also excludes the Civil War.

You can even put the Asian guy who shot up Virginia Tech in the "general racial minority" category, even though it dulls the point of historical injustice. Asians have suffered racial injustice big time, but as purposeful immigrants. American Indians are not immigrants and African-Americans were imported to serve whites.

Go ahead, use Professor Google. Make your own lists by your own standards.

How many minority mass killers targeted whites v. how many white mass killers targeted minorities?

"Patriotism" in the American context is fidelity to the constitutional principle of peaceful coexistence with others not like you, whether they are different in what they believe or different in how their bodies appear.

There is something cockamamie in the way white people deploy the term "patriotism" as a cudgel against African-Americans and against American Indians. This cudgel comes into play whenever the disfavored minorities do something to win the admiration of the American public. I am reminded of the jihad against the great Sac and Fox Olympian, Wa-Tho-Huk, also known as Jim Thorpe.

If I point out this inconsistent public discourse, I will of course be accused of "playing the race card," a term that entered the American political lexicon when OJ Simpson proved that a rich black man could buy as much "justice" in America as a rich white man. Google T. Cullen Davis.

And I still want to see Gabby Douglas, in whatever hairstyle makes her comfortable, on a Wheaties box.

This racial disparity in both discourse and body count is disturbing, but on a bigger world stage than the Olympics, another young girl has taken a leading role in the same war against intolerance, expressed in a more radical way than in the United States.

It is we sinful women
who come out raising the banner of truth
up against barricades of lies on the highways
who find stories of persecution piled on each threshold
who find that tongues which could speak have been severed.
---Kishwar Naheed (Urdu to English translation by Ruksana Ahmed)

In the time-suck that is Facebook, I have changed my profile picture to one of Malala Yousafzai. Besides improving the visual appeal of the page, what am I trying to accomplish?

Malala is a 15-year-old student from the Swat Valley in Pakistan, an area formerly ruled by the Taliban, Islamic fundamentalists who believe that educating girls is sinful. This policy, coming from God, is not negotiable. Enforcement of the policy is up to any devout Muslim, as the God the Taliban follow is apparently too puny to enforce its own rules.

Enforcement in areas infested by the Taliban has included burning of schools and throwing acid on girls seeking to study.

At age 11, Malala began a blog published in English and Urdu by the BBC called *Diary of a Pakistani Schoolgirl* under the *nom de plume* Gul Makai (Corn Flower). When the Taliban fled the Swat Valley, Malala's identity became common knowledge. Fluent in English, the girl appeared on British and American television advocating that Islam does not ban education of women.

What does this have to do with us?

In Afghanistan, American troops have been dying in the

longest war in the history of this nation. It began in 2001 when the Taliban refused to surrender the leader of Al Qaeda, Osama bin Laden.

Our troops ran the Taliban out of the cities and into the Pashtun tribal area along the Afghanistan/Pakistan border. The Taliban had the support of the Pakistani government until we started shooting at the Taliban and demanded that the Pakistanis choose a side.

While Pakistan ostensibly chose our side, the Taliban are still a potent political force. We've seen this movie before. Only the Pashtun people can root out the Taliban insanity. Not the Pakistani army, and certainly not the US army.

On October 9, 2012, a Taliban gunman attacked a school bus and shot Malala Yousafzai in the head. Two other girls were critically injured, but Malala was the target. "Malala was using her tongue and pen against Islam and Muslims," the Taliban said in a public statement through a media spokesman (such is their status that they have a media spokesman), "so she was punished for her crime by the blessing of the Almighty Allah."

So far, it appears that this crime has not received the blessing of the Pashtun people. Within the week, street demonstrations in Pakistani cities were displaying pictures of Malala.

Many years ago, world opinion was outraged when the Taliban destroyed ancient Buddhist statutes. The banning of television, sports, and music upset even local opinion. But by attempting to kill a young girl for the crime of wanting to go to school, the Taliban may finally have put themselves in a place where no decent person will shelter them. Hope springs eternal.

What does this have to do with me, other than the fact that my son is a GI?

I would hope that no man with daughters would ask that question. Both of my daughters are well educated, and I'm proud of them. Two of my granddaughters are in college right now. One granddaughter is a toddler with a twin brother. While I know I will not live to see what they become, I have dreams for them both, no greater for the boy than for the girl. And there is another granddaughter who is Malala's age.

I hate to trouble children with the existence of evil, but I hope my grandchildren will identify with Malala, with her courage and her ambition. They are Malala; all of our daughters are Malala.

And so I am Malala.

Malala's pen name, Gul Makai, comes from the heroine of a Pakistani folk tale, a Romeo and Juliet story, where the lovers meet at school. The romance between Gul Makai and her lover, Musa Khan, touches off a war between their tribes.

Gul Makai goes to the religious leaders and persuades them, by reference to the *Holy Quran,* that the grounds for the war are "frivolous." Inspired by the teachings of a girl, the leaders place themselves between the warring parties, holding the *Quran* over their heads, and persuade the two sides as Gul Makai has persuaded them. To seal the peace, the lovers are united in marriage.

According to the English translation by Masud-Ul-Hasan, "Most of the love stories generally have tragic ends; in the case of.... Musa Khan and Gul Makai... events took a different turn. The credit for this goes to Gul Makai. She did not rest content to love, and die. She was a woman of action; she loved, won, and lived."

As I write, the Pakistani government has committed to a national policy to educate girls, a policy pressed by the United Nations in Malala's name. Malala is in a British rehabilitation hospital with other veterans injured in the war with the Taliban, and a popular movement has arisen worldwide to make her the first child to win the Nobel Prize for Peace.

Until Gul Makai, Malala Yousafzai, the lover of knowledge, is out of the hospital, this old retired teacher will hide behind the face of a brave young girl. I am Malala.

18 LEGACY OF AN ELDER

Madeline Colliflower, known to her relatives as Si-Siya, walked on in her 81st year back in 2000, the cusp of the 21st century. She was one of few surviving FBI (Full Blooded Indian) citizens of the Gros Ventre.

Those of us who did not have the honor of knowing her personally should remember Colliflower for her arrest and conviction in the Fort Belknap Reservation Tribal Court that led to the enactment of the Indian Civil Rights Act. The Associated Press, noting Colliflower's passing, reported incorrectly that the Indian Civil Rights Act "guarantees defendants in tribal court the same rights provided in the U.S. Constitution."

The Indian Civil Rights Act is not a Bill of Rights for Indian Country. However, what happened to Colliflower is evidence that in fact Indian Country does need a Bill of Rights.

Colliflower was charged with disobeying a tribal court order to remove her cattle from land leased to another person. If guilty, she should have been punished. However, the tribal court judge who convicted her also prosecuted her. And she was convicted without being allowed to give evidence in her defense. Under those procedures, who knows if she was guilty?

Contrary to Anglo-American legal folklore, many civilized legal systems get along fine with the roles of judge and prosecutor, or at least investigator, combined. How about most of Western Europe, where a judge is in charge of the investigation, the judge is allowed to consider the defendant's failure to testify, and the trial does not begin until the judge is convinced that the defendant is probably guilty? Are all the civil tradition countries uncivilized? But not allowing Madeline Colliflower to defend herself is, pardon the expression, indefensible. Maybe the cattle were there without her knowledge. Maybe they were not in fact her cattle because she had sold them. Maybe she had an emergency on her land that made it necessary to move the cattle. We don't know these things even if we know that cattle with her brand were in the wrong place, and sorting such things out is why we have courts.

The question becomes what shall be done when a tribal court--or, for that matter, a chief or a tribal council--gets out of hand, does injustice, or violates fundamental human rights? Congress' response was the Indian Civil Rights Act of 1968. It purported to apply a slightly watered down version of the Bill of Rights to Indian Country. There are some rights that simply make no sense in the tribal context.

Freedom from establishment of religion is absolutely necessary for the United States, when so many of the original settlers came to these shores to escape religious persecution or to be free to visit religious persecution on others, depending on your point of view.

The right to counsel in criminal cases is imperfectly realized in the United States but out of the question on most Indian reservations, at least if "counsel" is understood to mean licensed attorneys.

Protection against "cruel and unusual punishment" is a completely culture-bound concept. In *Crow Dog's Case*, the tribal court would have found the American sentence cruel and unusual, because the tribal court had determined that Crow Dog posed no threat to the community and it was therefore un-necessary to kill him. A serious cruelty from the Indian point of view--banishment--excites little interest in American courts.

Culture clashes aside, allowing Indians to take their own tribal officials to federal court is an affront to Indian self-government. The only thing that keeps the Indian Civil Rights Act minimally palatable to the tribes is its lack of teeth. The only remedy for a violation is *habeas corpus*, which means that tribal governments can violate the Indian Civil Rights Act at will as long as they do not lock anyone up.

The Indian Civil Rights Act and the issues it raises are a

colossal good news and bad news joke for Indian sovereignty.

Few tribes ever had any reason to develop a concept of individual rights enforceable against the tribe. This is a concept only necessary to govern heterogeneous cultures, like the U.S. It has become necessary to govern Indian nations because of Christianity and other outside influences, and if the Indian nations do not develop self-governing means to rein in dishonest or tyrannical officials, the U.S. government will be more than happy to do it for us.

Instead, whenever some dishonesty or tyranny happens within an Indian government, our leaders line up to wave the bloody red shirt of sovereignty.

One major tribe was only able to remove a corrupt chief after federal indictment because the chief did not allow tribal citizens to have access to the voting lists. Did this glaring bit of tyranny get reformed by the new administration? No. Sovereignty is a shield to incumbency, whether the incumbent is a crook or not.

Indian sovereignty lies in tatters already. What remains of sovereignty ought to be insufficient to shield dishonesty and tyranny, even if there were some advantage for Indians in being ruled by crooks. I am reminded of Vine Deloria, Jr.'s *bon mot* that Indians vote for crooks and white people vote for morons.

Should the Indian Civil Rights be expanded to allow lawsuits in federal court whenever tribal governments violate individual rights? No. But if tribal governments continue to steal from their own people and then hide behind sovereignty, the day will come when there is no sovereignty left to hide behind. We must develop tribal understandings of individual rights, and tribal mechanisms to vindicate those rights.

Having this conversation, not the Indian Civil Rights Act, would be a more fitting memorial to the Gros Ventre elder Madeline Colliflower, Si-Siya.

19 MEET THE FATHER OF AMERICAN INDIAN CONTROL LAW

Once upon a time, in the late 20th and early 21st centuries, there was a patriotic organization of lawyers and academics, the Federalist Society. They were alarmed by federal court decisions that appeared to favor non-white persons and to prefer human persons over corporate persons.

Over the years, they gained virtual veto power over judicial appointments by one of the major political parties and they opened chapters in every major law school, to catch new lawyers before deviant ideas could take hold. By 2012, four justices of the Supreme Court were Federalist Society members---Antonin Scalia, Clarence Thomas, John Roberts, and Samuel Alito.

They preached that the "plain language" of the Constitution in light of the "original intent" of the Founders could answer all constitutional questions. Their hero was one of the Founders, the first great Chief Justice of the United States, the Federalist John Marshall....

Picture a Presidential election that makes the Bush and Gore 2000 election appear to be politics-as-usual and you have some approximation of the 1800 election.

One party, the Federalists, had controlled the US government since the revolution. Modern history teaches us that the acid test of a revolution comes not in seizing power, but in governance and the peaceful transition of that power to legitimate successors. The king is dead; long live the king. In 1800, there had been other revolutions but there were no role models.

The Alien and Sedition Acts had been used against critics of the government, the Democratic-Republicans. Let's be clear: people were locked up for criticizing the government. Still, newspapers of the day were as biased as Fox News in our times, and they were willing to sling any mud handy and make up some if mud were scarce.

George Washington, the military hero of the revolution, had declined the open opportunity to rule for his biological life, King George I of the Americas replacing King George III of England. His chosen successor, John Adams, faced unrelenting attacks by the intellectual father of the Democratic-Republicans, today's Democratic Party, Thomas Jefferson.

In those days, the President was the winner of a plurality in the Electoral College and the Vice President was the man who came in second, regardless of party. There were slates, of course, and the Democratic-Republican slate was Jefferson for President and Aaron Burr for Vice President.

Jefferson and Burr tied in the Electoral College, sending the election to the House of Representatives, as some expected might happen with the Bush and Gore election in 2000.

In the House, Jefferson's difficulty became not Adams but Burr, who lacked the party loyalty to put his support behind Jefferson. Burr could deny Jefferson the nine of sixteen states required to win, and Burr would not back down.

While the House voted and re-voted without result, the deadline to seat a new President came and went. This led the Adams supporters to float the legal position that because no successor had been lawfully qualified, Adams was still President for another term and the attempted election was moot. Pennsylvania and Virginia mobilized their militias, and the American Revolution appeared doomed.

The Federalists blinked and threw enough of their support to Jefferson (the lesser of the evils by their lights) to deny the presidency to Burr after 36 deadlocked ballots. This placing of country before party did not, however, mean an end to bad feelings from the nasty and personal campaign.

Adams and the lame duck Federalist Congress set about entrenching as much Federalist power as possible in the waning days of his administration. Congress created judgeships to be appointed by Adams and therefore denied to Jefferson. This is where our political lexicon gained the phrase "midnight appointments."

One of these midnight appointments was the Federalist Secretary of State, John Marshall, to be Chief Justice of the United States, a lifetime appointment he assumed while still functioning as Secretary of State. Another went to a lowly justice of the peace, one William Marbury.

Jefferson was predictably outraged and instructed his newly appointed Secretary of State, James Madison, to withhold commissions from as many midnight appointees as possible.

Marbury, who was denied his commission, sued James Madison in the Supreme Court for a writ of *mandamus* ordering Madison to deliver it. Chief Justice John Marshall had, as Secretary of State, been responsible for the fact that the commission was not delivered in the first place. That would seem an ethical bar to Marshall sitting on the case, since his impartiality appeared compromised, but these were different times. Marshall's impartiality would be as questionable by modern standards later, when he crafted one of the foundational decisions in federal Indian law.

Jefferson held a view of the Constitution now dismissed by all but Newt Gingrich: that Congress and the President and the Supreme Court all have a duty to interpret the Constitution but none have authority to require the other branches to comply with their interpretation, except that the President has the army and the Congress has the purse and the Supreme Court has...nothing but the persuasion of a well written opinion.

The expected scenario was that the Federalist Marshall would rule in favor of the Federalist Marbury and the Democratic-Republicans Jefferson and Madison would invite Marshall to urinate up a rope. This would end the controversy, although plainly it could cause many others.

Marshall had nothing but his wits, which were more than up to the task, and this is why American Indians caught in the webs he wove should never underestimate his ability. We can learn from his writings that every legal blade has at least two edges.

Marshall asked whether the common law entitled Marbury to a writ of *mandamus*, an order requiring an officer to act? It plainly did. Marbury's appointment was a discretionary act, which cannot be the subject of *mandamus*. A court could not order the President whom to appoint. But the delivery of Marbury's commission was a mere ministerial act, involving no discretion, and this situation is the very stuff of *mandamus.*

So Marbury won the lawsuit and Jefferson refused to enforce the decision, right? Just like Andrew Jackson would later refuse to enforce *Worchester v. Georgia* and send my people on the Trail of Tears?

Wrong. The Supreme Court's authority to issue the writ of *mandamus,* Marshall opined, was based on the Judiciary Act of 1789. That act conflicted with the jurisdiction of the Court set out in the Constitution *AND WAS THEREFORE VOID*, what we call today "unconstitutional." In our times, the word "unconstitutional" is thrown around routinely in all sorts of political debates, but in Marshall's time the power of a court to overrule Congress was not at all as clear as Marshall made it sound.

Jefferson, nobody's fool, saw the power Marshall had arrogated to the Court, and was fit to be tied. But what could he do or say? He had won the case on the merits. He won the right to appoint his own justice of the peace and lost a critical point of constitutional theory that lives to our times, when the Supreme Court found the Florida recount in 2000 to be "unconstitutional" and handed the election to the political descendants of Marshall at the expense of the political descendants of Jefferson.

John Marshall went on to be the longest serving Chief Justice in US history, but he never again used the power he had crafted against an act of Congress. Overruling Congress, remember, came in the midst of an election dispute that threatened civil war. The second use of the power was by Marshall's successor, Roger Taney, in *Dred Scott v. Sandford,* and it did indeed touch off a civil war.

All Americans should know the story of *Marbury v. Madison,* but few do.

All American Indians should know the story for a whole other set of reasons.

John Marshall, the architect of *Marbury* who used it to arrogate the power of judicial review from next to nothing is also the man who, in three seminal cases, crafted the foundations of federal Indian law from next to nothing. Those foundations would, long after Marshall had gone to his reward, support the arrogation of "plenary power" to Congress over Indian nations.

Before he set about the task of constructing what most academics call federal Indian law but many Indian academics call federal Indian *control* law, Marshall made clear that the same power to overrule unconstitutional laws applied to the states. In *Fletcher v. Peck* (1810), Marshall's Supreme Court declared unconstitutional Georgia's attempt to rescind the sale of lands ancestral to the Cherokee and Creek peoples (among others) in spite of the fact that virtually the entire Georgia legislature had been bribed to accomplish the sale in the first place.

Indians were bystanders in *Fletcher v. Peck*, but they did get sideswiped when Marshall wrote "the majority of the court is of the opinion that the nature of the Indian title, which is certainly to be respected by all courts, until it be legitimately extinguished, is not such as to be absolutely repugnant to… (state ownership)."

Indians were hit head-on thirteen years later, in a Marshall opinion full of imagined facts, made-up law, and ethical questions. This was *Johnson v. M'intosh*, the first case in the three-legged stool that supports all of modern Indian law.

The nature of Indian right, Marshall opined, was the right of occupancy, not ownership. This finding rested principally on his apprehension that Europeans were Christians and Indians were not. At this time, the *Book of Mormon* had not yet revealed that Jesus Christ visited North America.

One imagined fact was that all Indians were hunter-gatherers when Europeans showed up. Marshall was innocent of the Cahokia Mounds, Chaco Canyon, and other physical evidence of sedentary peoples with substantial agricultural surplus, but he should have been familiar with the Six Nations and the Cherokee, both of which produced agricultural surplus at the time of the European invasion.

Probably the most famous words from *Johnson v. M'intosh* are after the assumption that the "savages" (his word) were not farmers: "We will not enter into the controversy whether agriculturists, merchants, and manufacturers have a right on abstract principles to expel hunters from the territory they possess or to contract their limits. *Conquest gives a title which the courts of the conqueror cannot deny…*"

This blunt statement was really in our best interests, because "…the tribes of Indians inhabiting this country were fierce savages whose occupation was war and whose subsistence was drawn chiefly from the forest. To leave them in possession of their country was to leave the country a wilderness…" Everyone knows wilderness is not of any use.

An ethical question arises from this opinion in our times because the legal issue was whether title granted by the US government was superior to title granted by an Indian tribe, and the answer was that the US government title prevailed. John Marshall and his immediate family, at the time, claimed over half a million acres of land under the same chain of title his opinion endorsed. In modern times, we call that a conflict of interest and we don't let the judge hear the case. The conflict could have been repaired if Marshall had ruled against his own interests---but he did not.

In 1831, Marshall finally laid out, in so many words, the constitutional status of Indian nations. The state of Georgia had passed acts nullifying Cherokee laws on Cherokee land and providing, among other things, that Indians were not competent to testify in Georgia courts. The Cherokee Nation sued Georgia in the Supreme Court to stop this.

The Supreme Court has authority to hear cases between states or states and a foreign state. In *Cherokee Nation v. Georgia*, Marshall decided that the Cherokee Nation was not a "foreign state" but rather a "domestic, dependent nation," and therefore could not bring the lawsuit.

However, one of the anti-Indian laws passed by the state of Georgia required white people residing within the Cherokee Nation to get a license from the state. Samuel Worcester, a Baptist missionary, refused to get a state license and as a result was sentenced to four years at hard labor. The Cherokee Nation took up his defense as a method of raising the same issues Marshall had turned away in *Cherokee Nation v. Georgia*.

Reaching the merits this time in *Worcester v. Georgia*, Marshall held that the Cherokee Nation had inherent sovereignty such that Georgia had no authority to nullify Cherokee laws and Georgia laws had no force within the Cherokee Nation. Some historians believe that Marshall had watched in horror as his opinions in *Fletcher* and *Johnson* were cited as justification for the oppression he decisively rejected in *Worcester*.

Justice Joseph Story, probably Marshall's most distinguished colleague on the Supreme Court, wrote in a letter to his wife in 1832: "Thanks be to God, the Court can wash their hands clean of the iniquity of oppressing the Indians and disregarding their rights."

While the justices may have thought their hands needed washing, President Andrew Jackson had no such queasiness about violating Indian rights, and all of the Southeastern tribes had their own trails of tears. My people just named it, and lost more citizens on the way to Indian Territory.

John Marshall built the foundations for a claim of "plenary power" over Indian property, although subsequent courts had to get around the respect for Indian treaties Marshall expressed in his *Worcester* opinion.

In an ironic twist, Congress's failure to discharge the obligations imposed by plenary power, combined with the authority that spins out of *Marbury*, has laid the most odious recent colonial usurpations of federal Indian law at the door not of Congress, the possessor of the power, but of the Supreme Court, the creator of it.

In our times, there is more Indian fighting on the Supreme Court than in Congress, weaving more policy from the threads originally spun by the brilliant old Federalist, John Marshall.

THE POWER OF JOHN MARSHALL'S PEN AT A GLANCE:

The Constitution (1787) said about the power of the Supreme Court:

Article III, Section 1
The judicial Power of the United States, shall be vested in one supreme Court, and in such inferior Courts as the Congress may from time to time ordain and establish...

John Marshall wrote about the power of the Supreme Court:

Marbury v. Madison, 5 U.S. 137 (1803). The Supreme Court has the power to declare acts of Congress void for being "repugnant to" the Constitution, what we now call "unconstitutional."

91

Fletcher v. Peck, 10 U.S. 87 (1810). The Supreme Court has the power to declare state laws unconstitutional.

The Constitution said about Indians:

Article I, Section 2
The House of Representatives shall be composed of Members chosen every second Year by the People of the several States.... Representatives and direct Taxes shall be apportioned among the several States which may be included within this Union, according to their respective Numbers, which shall be determined by adding to the whole Number of free Persons, including those bound to Service for a Term of Years, and excluding Indians not taxed, three fifths of all other Persons.

Article I, Section 8
The Congress shall have Power...To regulate Commerce with foreign Nations, and among the several States, and with the Indian Tribes.

John Marshall wrote about Indians:

Johnson v. M'Intosh, 21 U.S. 543 (1823). Indians do not own the land beneath their feet, but rather have a right of occupancy that may only be extinguished by the United States. This is based on the Doctrine of Discovery, understood to mean the right of Christians to take the property of non-Christians.

Cherokee Nation v. Georgia, 30 U.S. 1 (1831). Indian nations are not foreign states that can bring lawsuits in the Supreme Court, but rather "domestic, dependent nations."

Worcester v. Georgia, 31 U.S. (6 Pet.) 515 (1832). Indian nations have inherent sovereignty, which includes the right to make laws for their own governance, and state laws have no force on Indian land.

20 CALLING FOR AN INDIAN THESEUS

Should Indians allow non-Indians to vote when they reside on Indian land and are affected by the outcome of the election? The instinctive reaction is "No way!" and defending that reaction is so simple it's hard to understand the charge of unfairness.

I've chosen to live in Texas, but my roots still reach into Oklahoma and I spend a lot of time there. Suppose I hit a lottery number and could finally acquire the cabin on Lake Tenkiller that has always occupied a prominent spot in my dreams? Should I then be able to claim a vote in Oklahoma as well as a vote in Texas?

For federal election purposes, the question answers itself. To let me choose delegates to the Electoral College in both Texas and Oklahoma would certainly benefit John McCain, who I think finally decided he has eight houses. It would also benefit Willard Mitt Romney of Massachusetts, New Hampshire, Michigan, Utah, and California. But that's not the rule. One federal vote to a citizen is the rule. We no longer have to own real estate to be voters, but I had to bring up my would-be cabin on Tenkiller to make the scenario credible.

We don't object that passing though another state subject to the traffic laws of that state gives us no right to vote there, nor do we claim that paying the sales tax in another state makes us subject to "taxation without representation."

Given this daily experience for most US citizens, I cannot understand the objection to being bound by tribal laws on tribal

93

land. On the contrary, it seems strange to me that in my recent road trip that touched half a dozen Indian nations, I was fully subject to the laws of the lands I visited while my brother—who has an identical Cherokee blood quantum but has not chosen dual citizenship in the Cherokee Nation—was not.

If we drive into another state, we don't consider it a big deal to ask whether right turns on red are allowed. I note that some New Mexico pueblos post a big billboard admonishing the people who enter the pueblo that they are submitting to tribal jurisdiction. The fact is not odd, but the fact that the tribe finds it necessary to announce the existence of tribal law is.

All that understood, why should a tribe not allow non-citizens to vote on certain questions or on all questions if the tribe thinks that is they way their land should be governed?

Within my own tribe, I continually ask similar questions.

Why should we not have a poll tax, at least for outlanders such as myself?

Why should ballots not be printed in Cherokee? Only.

Why should we not levy an income tax on outlanders only?

No Indian nation is the same as it was, and some of the changes we did not choose. We survivors should not fear change, because it has been key to our survival.

According to the Greeks, a fellow named Procrustes violated the tradition of hospitality to travelers by offering them a very special bed that fit nobody. If they were too short for the bed, Procrustes would break their legs and stretch them to fit. If they were too tall, some amputation was done.

We treat the US Constitution as if it were a Procrustean bed and we force our tribal laws to conform to it. Speaking from utmost respect for the Constitution, I say that is dangerous nonsense.

The Constitution was written for peoples who were not united by geography, ethnicity, language, religion, or any other customary social glue. The US is what Benedict Anderson has called an "imagined community," and it's the first one in history to be wildly successful. The Constitution deserves credit for that, but Indian nations are not "imagined communities." Indian nations are real communities. We have been all about social glue, and our task in governing is to preserve that glue.

Poll taxes and literacy tests were evil in the US context,

enacted for the purpose of keeping former slaves powerless. Unlike the US, certain tribes may have good reason to make non-residents jump more hoops or to let non-citizens vote.

The story of Procrustes represents an order where people do what they are told or act as they always have without question. Theseus is the Greek hero who slew Procrustes and founded what Europeans incorrectly believe was the first democracy in Athens.

Pre-Columbian Indians had the knack for political theory. The size of indigenous civilizations proves it. The political challenges we face are not of our making, but the solutions will be unless we have lost that knack. It's good to be schooled in US law, but solutions to tribal governance issues are in the tradition of Theseus rather than Procrustes.

I've heard many Indian activist friends ask why there is no American Indian Martin Luther King, Jr. or Cesar Chavez? Having generated the artistic and intellectual foundations for the rise of such a leader, it's fair to ask that question.

Indian nations have failed in the past to unite around leaders of a violent resistance. Now they need to unite in a nonviolent resistance to remain distinct peoples with more identity than romantic national mascots.

Seizing the power of self-government, daunting as the difficulty appears, pales in comparison to the challenge of using that power. For that, we need an Indian Theseus. Or five hundred of them.

ABOUT THE AUTHOR

Steve Russell is a citizen of the Cherokee Nation, born and raised in the Creek Nation. He dropped out of Bristow, Oklahoma High School in the ninth grade.

After serving in the U.S. Air Force from 1964 to 1968, he graduated *magna cum laude* from the University of Texas at Austin, and went on to earn a law degree from the same school. He also received a master of judicial studies degree from the University of Nevada at Reno.

His first career was as a Texas trial court judge, first on the Austin Municipal Court and then Travis County Court at Law No. Two.

His second career was as a criminal justice professor, first at the University of Texas at San Antonio and then at Indiana University, Bloomington. He is currently Associate Professor *Emeritus* of Criminal Justice at Indiana University and retains his judicial status in Texas as well.

Twice retired, Russell lives with his wife Tracy in Georgetown, Texas. He writes a regular column on tribal affairs for *Indian Country Today*.

Russell is the author of *Sequoyah Rising: Problems in Post-Colonial Tribal Governance* (Carolina Academic Press (2010) and *Wicked Dew* (Dog Iron Press 2012), winner of the Poetry First Book Award from the Native Writers Circle of the Americas in 2008.